Construction Competences for NVQ Level 2

Bricklaying

By the same author:

Brickwork 1
Brickwork 2
Brickwork 3
Brickwork Bonding Problems and Solutions
Brickwork Repair and Restoration

Construction Competences for NVQ Level 2

BRICKLAYING

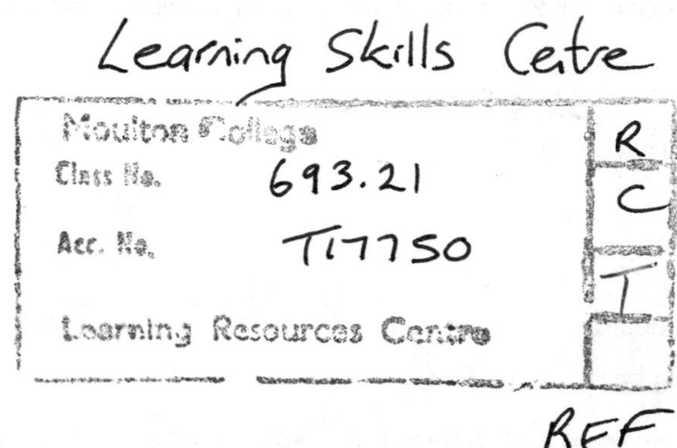

W.G. Nash, MCIOB

First published in 1991 by:
Stanley Thornes (Publishers) Ltd

Reprinted in 2002 by:
Nelson Thornes Ltd
Delta Place
27 Bath Road
CHELTENHAM
GL53 7TH
United Kingdom

04 05 06 07 / 10 9 8 7

A catalogue record for this book is available from the British Library

ISBN 0 7487 1292 5

Page make-up by Tech-Set Ltd

Printed and bound in Great Britain by Athenaeum Press

Contents

National Vocational Qualifications – NVQs vi

Introduction viii

How to use this package ix

1. Bricklaying basics 1
Safe methods of working 2
Tools 5
Bricks 9
Mortars 11
Bonding 13

2. Solid brick walls 17
Methods of working 17
Bonds for solid brick walls 22
Setting out 30
Damp-proofing 32
Copings 36
Parapet walls 39
Reinforced brickwork 41
Bridging openings 43

3. Half-brick walls 45
Stretcher bond 45
Openings in half-brick walling 49
Cutting to a rake 53

4. Isolated and attached piers 55
Isolated piers 55
Attached piers 58
Jointing 61

5. Blockwork 64
Blocks 64
Building blockwork 67
Openings in blockwork 73

6. Cavity walls 74
Cavity walling 74
Openings in cavity walls 79
Cavity insulation 85

7. Chimney breasts, flues and stacks 87
Chimneys and flues 87
Chimney construction 94

Index 99

National vocational qualifications – NVQs

The work of a skilled person in the construction industry can be divided into various tasks, e.g. build a brick wall, paint a ceiling, hang a door, etc. These tasks along with many others are called **Units of Competence**. They can be considered as a 'menu' for selection by yourself on a 'pick and mix' basis according to your requirements.

Traditional barriers to gaining a qualification such as age, length of training, mode of training, how and where skills are acquired, have been removed. You may train for NVQs in any order as, when and where you want.

Credits for Units of Competence which can be accumulated over any period of time, may be built into an NVQ award at three levels:

NVQ Level 1	Introduction to industry, a 'foundation' common core plus craft-specific basic skills.
NVQ Level 2	A subset of Units of Competence in a recognisable work role, e.g. bench joinery, site carpentry, etc.
NVQ Level 3	A set number of relevant Units of Competence in a chosen occupational area of work, including supervisory studies, e.g. carpenter and joiner, bricklayer, etc.

NVQ qualifications in construction are jointly awarded by City and Guilds of London Institute (CGLI) and Construction Industry Training Board (CITB).

Prior achievement

It is not always necessary to undertake training for every Unit of Competence as colleges and other accredited centres will in future be able to undertake **Accreditation of Prior Learning/Achievement** (**APL/A**). Through this process it is possible to gain credits for Units of Competence which have either formed part of another course you have studied, or tasks you have previously carried out in industry.

You will need to produce evidence of the competence from past performance. This would then be taken into account when determining your training/accreditation programme and for the award of a qualification.

The advantages of this process are:

- increased motivation of trainees because there is no duplication of training previously carried out
- easier access to qualifications for experienced and mature trainees who have not had the opportunity to demonstrate their competences earlier.

A guide for lecturers, instructors and supervisors ('tutors')

An NVQ programme is unit based, it needs to be flexible so that an employer or individual can specify a training and accreditation programme specifically to their requirements. Set length courses will become a thing of the past and a 'roll-on/roll-off' system of independent competency units, packaged according to employer or individual needs will come to the fore. Each unit is intended to be entirely free-standing with no prescribed order of attainment, time duration or start time. Therefore trainees with widely differing abilities and undertaking varying units, will have to be accommodated by the 'tutor'.

A trainee-centred learning approach using learning packages supported by tutor reinforcement and guidance is the ideal answer. It enables a flexible learning programme which caters for self selection, individual progression, mixed ability and 'roll-on/roll-off' programmes.

Using this method the trainees are made responsible for their own learning, which is task orientated. The tutor's role changes to one of a facilitator, counsellor and assessor.

Construction Competences for NVQ Level 2 – Bricklaying is one of the building craft competence series of craft/level specific packages which should be used in conjunction with *A Building Craft 'Foundation'* by Peter Brett to provide a resource base for the implementation of NVQ Building Craft programmes within your training environment. In addition to these packages a tutor's guide is available which gives advice on learning strategies and provides answers to the trainee tasks undertaken.

Introduction

The learning package which you are about to start is one of the Construction Competences for NVQ Level 2: Bricklaying. Once successfully completed it forms part of an NVQ Level 2 occupational award. In order to obtain the full NVQ Level 2 occupational award, you must also successfully complete the NVQ Common Core.

The following six units make up the NVQ Level 2 Bricklaying:

Unit 044 Constructing Solid Brick Walls
Unit 045 Constructing Half Brick Walls
Unit 046 Constructing Isolated and Attached Piers
Unit 047 Constructing Blockwork
Unit 048 Constructing Cavity Walls
Unit 049 Constructing Chimney Breasts, Flues and Stacks

The enthusiastic trainee who wishes to pursue the topics contained in this package in greater detail is recommended to refer to *Brickwork 1* and *Brickwork 2* by the same author.

How to use this package

This is a self-study package designed to be supported by:

- tutor reinforcement and guidance
- group discussion
- films, slides and videos.

You should read/work through each section of a unit, one at a time as required. Discuss its content with your group, tutor, or friends wherever possible. Attempt to answer the *Questions for you* in that section. Progressively read through all the sections, discussing them and answering the questions as you go.

This process is intended to aid learning and enable you to evaluate your understanding of the particular section and to check your progress through the units and entire package. Where you are unable to answer a question, further reading and discussion of the section is required.

Throughout this learning package 'Harry' the general foreman and his thoughts will prompt you to undertake an activity or task.

The *Questions for you* in this package are either multiple choice or short answer.

Multiple-choice questions consist of a statement or question followed by four possible answers. Only **one** answer is correct, the others are distractors. Your response is recorded by filling in the line under the appropriate letter.

Example

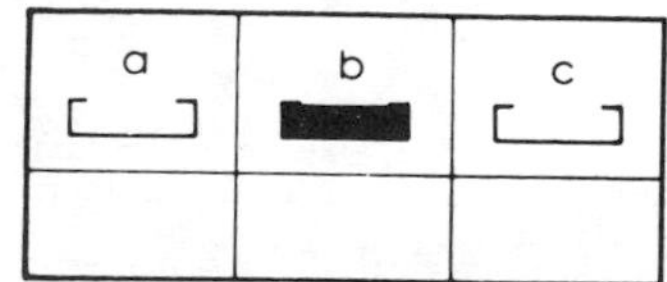

This indicates that you have selected (b) as the answer.

If after consideration you want to change your mind, fill in the box under your first answer and then fill in the line under the new letter.

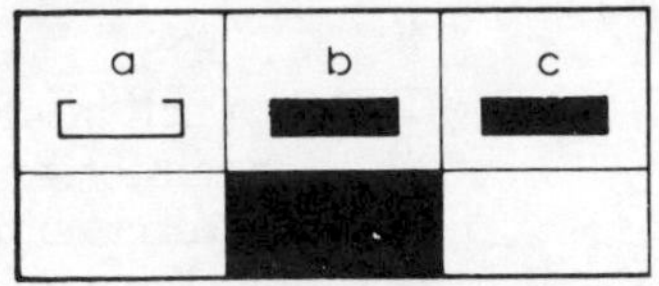

This changes the answer from (b) to (c).

Short-answer questions consist of a task to which a short written answer is required. The length will vary depending on the 'doing' word in the task, **Name** or **List** normally require one or two words for each item, **State**, **Define**, **Describe** or **Explain** will require a short sentence. In certain cases a labelled sketch may be all that is required.

Example

Name the architect's on-site representative.

Typical answer: The clerk of works.

Example

Define the term 'the building team'.

Typical answer: The team of professionals who work together to produce the required building or structure. Consists of the following parties: client, architect, quantity surveyor, specialist engineers, clerk of works, local authority health and safety inspector, building contractor, sub-contractors and material suppliers.

Example

Make a sketch to show the difference in size between a brick and a block.

Typical answer:

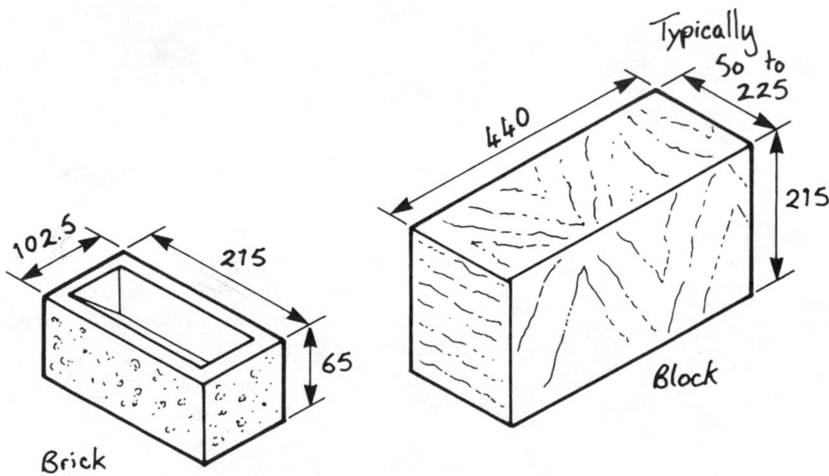

1 Bricklaying basics

Since the beginning of life, as we understand it, man has had to find shelter in order to protect himself from the elements and even from other forms of life. Thus builders were among the original craftsmen and many sophisticated systems of construction have evolved over the centuries. Nevertheless, in spite of the differing styles and methods of building there are still basic principles of craftsmanship which have to be thoroughly understood and practised. This will always be the case, since without craftsmen the industry would not survive.

When skilled people are working, their operations seem to be simple and easy to understand, but much practice is needed in order to produce work which is not only of a high standard but also carried out in an economic manner. This book is intended to highlight those basic principles and to assist you, the reader, to achieve a high standard of craftsmanship of which you can be justly proud, and which will allow you to work with complete confidence in any situation of your choice.

Safe methods of working

It is most important that all work is carried out in a safe manner and that due regard is made to one's own safety as well as that of other people who may be working in adjacent situations. The construction industry, by its very nature, can be a very dangerous one, but if everyone takes adequate safety precautions at all times then the industry can become a much safer one in which to work.

The following precautions should always be observed.

- The wearing of *protective clothing* such as helmets, goggles when cutting away with a hammer and chisel, and safety shoes or boots with steel toecaps is essential.
- Mortar boards are often placed on bricks to reduce the amount of bending when picking up the mortar. In these cases, the boards must be supported at each corner in order to avoid traps which could cause a person to over-balance if he or she accidently stepped on it. Figure 1.1 shows a suitable layout for a mortar board and the placing of bricks.

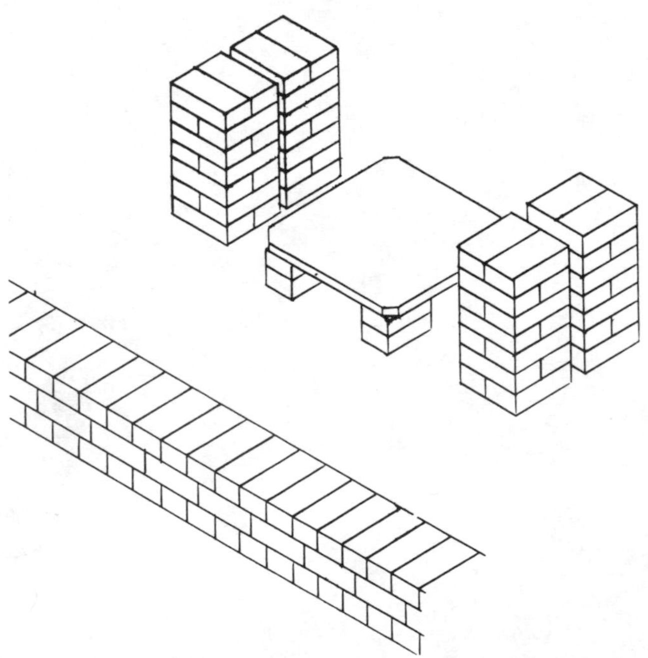

Figure 1.1 Typical layout of a mortar board and bricks

- The working space between the mortar boards and walling should be kept completely clear of debris or tools which may cause a person to stumble.
- When stacking bricks on a raised scaffold they should be placed as near as possible to a standard or vertical member of the scaffold, rather than in between the standards. In no case, however, must a scaffold be overloaded with bricks or any other materials which may cause a hazard.
- Do not indulge in any foolhardy practices which may endanger yourself or any other person.

Using electrical equipment

There are some basic rules regarding the use of electrical equipment which, if followed at all times, could help prevent a large number of accidents.

- Always ensure that proper industrial plugs and sockets are used for the wiring of the machines. These are rubber-covered and prevent the penetration of water.
- Whilst the operator may not have any control over the type of equipment he is expected to use, nevertheless, only low-voltage machines should be used on sites. These are usually run from transformers which should be carefully looked after and placed in a safe place when in use. Equipment requiring 240 volts should not be used on a site as it could be lethal if a break should occur in the wiring.
- The wiring should be provided with an automatic circuit breaker which will cut off the current if there is any accidental cutting of the wire. This will safeguard the operator from being electrocuted.
- Before using any electrical appliance it is sound practice to check that
  1) the correct voltage is being used.
  2) there are no breaks or visible damage in the wiring.
  3) the sockets are sound and firmly in place.
  4) the wiring is kept clear of water.
  5) the grinder wheels or drills are firmly held in the chuck and thoroughly tightened with the aid of the chuck key.

Using brick-cutting machinery

When using brick-cutting machinery the following safety measures should be adopted:

- Ensure that the wiring to the machine has been correctly connected.
- Safety goggles must be worn to give full protection to the eyes.
- When using a stationary brick-cutting saw the operator should wear a rubber apron, since the blades of these machines are sprayed with water when running.
- If a portable angle grinder is used then special care must be taken when using this equipment to make certain that both hands are used to handle the machine in order to prevent them from coming into contact with the blade.
- When using an angle grinder the operator should wear a face mask to safeguard him from breathing in the dry dust.
- Safety footwear with steel toecaps is particularly recommended to guard the feet against injury if the grinder is accidently dropped.
- Be especially careful to keep the electric wiring away from the cutting disc to avoid accidental damage to the wiring.

Questions for you

1. It is important to learn the basic principles of craftsmanship:
(a) to earn more money
(b) to be able to adapt more easily to changing methods of working
(c) to be able to work on a bigger site

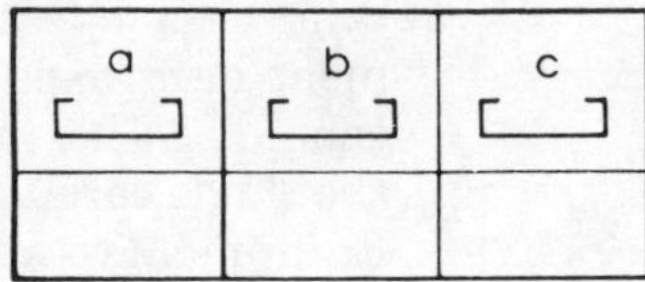

2. Good safety measures should be adopted on a site:
(a) to cut down on providing first aid equipment
(b) to avoid accidents
(c) they are a waste of time

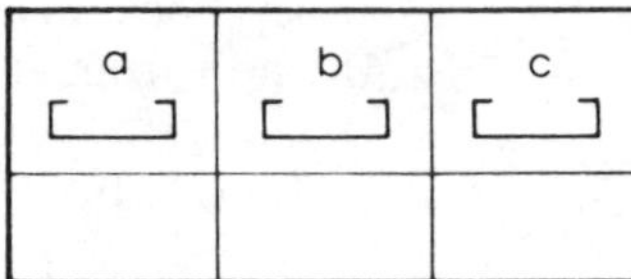

3. State **FOUR** basic safety measures that a craftsman should adopt.

____

____

____

____

4. When stacking bricks on a scaffold it is better to place them
(a) adjacent to a vertical scaffold member or standard
(b) between the standards
(c) anywhere on the platform

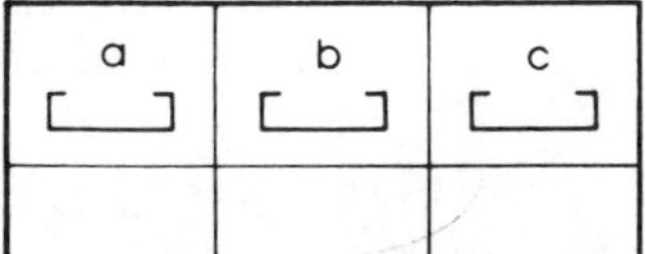

Tools

Before purchasing any tools it is best to seek advice from a well-known or respected craftsman who can give guidance as to which ones to buy. It is not generally sound practice to buy cheap DIY items which might satisfy the requirements of a handyman for an odd job but will not stand up to years of wear for a craftsman. As a rule, always buy good quality items.

The tools required include the following:

A trowel. Various sizes and shapes are available so select one that 'feels right' when you handle it. A 250 to 275 mm length blade would be suitable for most general work (Figure 1.2).

A pointing trowel. These are also available in various sizes but one with a blade length about 125 to 150 mm would be generally suitable.

A club hammer weighing 1 kg would be adequate for general purposes (Figure 1.3).

A bolster or boaster is used in conjunction with the club hammer for cutting bricks. These are available from 75 to 115 mm (Figure 1.4). Some bolsters are provided with a plastic or rubber cover at the head of the bolster to prevent the hands from being hurt by the mushroom head which forms at the top. It is good practice to remove the mushroom head from time to time with the aid of a grinder. A bolster should not be allowed to get too blunt so it should be sharpened occasionally on a grinder.

A cold chisel is used in conjunction with the club hammer for cutting holes and chases. A chisel can quickly become blunt if it is used to any great extent. Therefore it should be heated and drawn out from time to time to keep it sharpened. It is also a good idea to grind off the mushroom head at intervals and to use a plastic or rubber cover to protect the hands.

A pair of line pins and line (Figure 1.5).

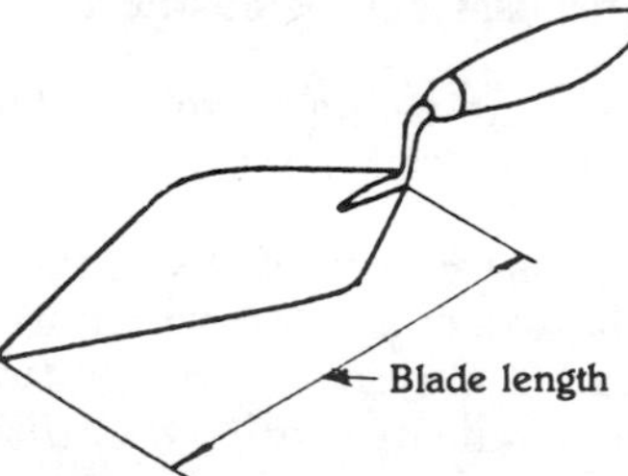

Figure 1.2 Brick trowel

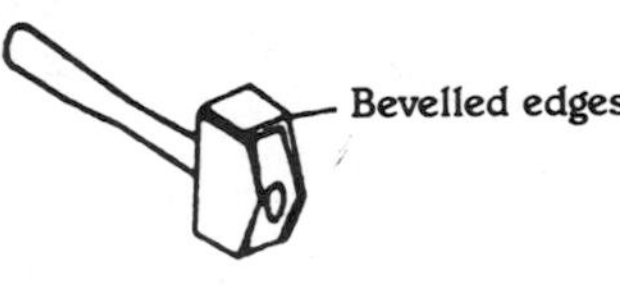

Figure 1.3 Club hammer

Figure 1.4 Bolster or boaster

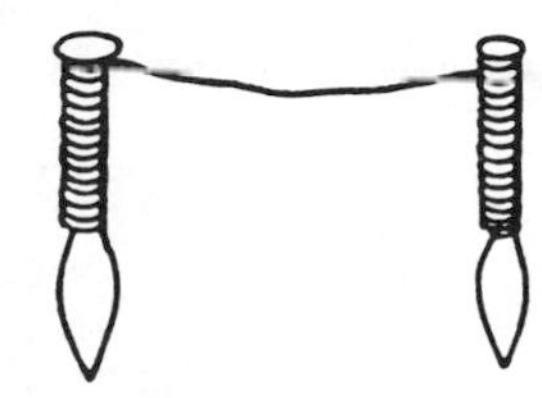

Figure 1.5 Line and pins

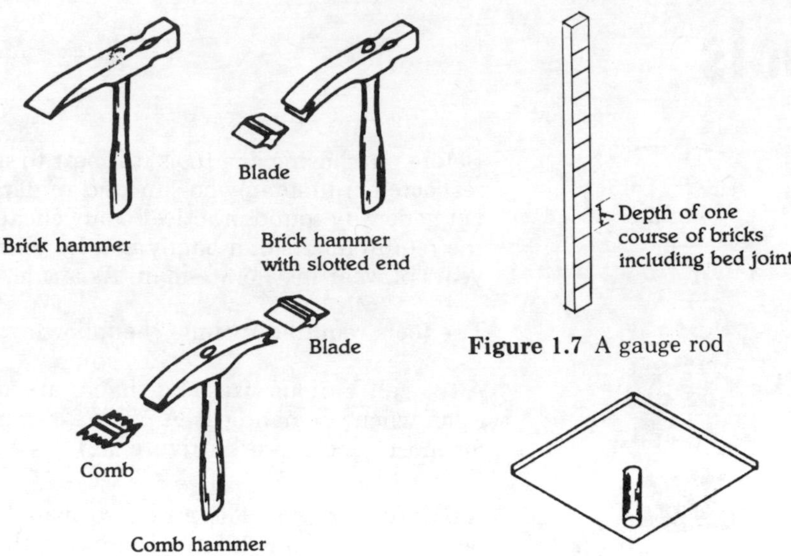

Figure 1.6 Types of hammers

Figure 1.7 A gauge rod

Figure 1.8 A hawk

A spirit level. These are available in various lengths but one about 900 mm long would be quite suitable for general work.

A comb hammer or brick hammer is used for trimming the bricks when they have been cut with the hammer and bolster. The comb hammer is used with blades which are discarded when worn out and then replaced with new ones (Figure 1.6).

A rule or measuring tape.

A gauge rod is used to check the height of the courses so that they all climb at a constant height (Figure 1.7). Though it may be of any required measurement, a gauge of four courses to 305 mm is usually quite suitable for general brickwork. The gauge rod can cut to any convenient length to suit the user's requirements, from about 900 mm long to a storey height of about three metres.

A hawk is used for carrying mortar when pointing (see p. 61). Such a tool may be purchased from a tool shop but one which would be quite suitable for general purposes can be easily made as shown in Figure 1.8.

A jointing iron can be made from a short length of reinforcing rod. This is used to give the brick joints a rounded finish (Figure 1.9).

A closer gauge is easily made by fixing one piece of batten across another to indicate the size of a *closer* which is a quarter of the length of a brick. The closer gauge may have an additional piece of batten fixed to the opposite side to indicate a *half bat* or *three-quarter bat*, which are half and three quarters the length of a brick respectively. This tool is extremely useful when working on facework where all the cut bricks have to be of consistent lengths. The bricks can be marked off easily with the aid of a gauge shown in Figure 1.10.

Corner blocks are easily made and are very useful when one does not wish to put line pins into the wall joints (Figure 1.11). The blocks are held in position by the line which is pulled taut and wound round the screws at the back of the block. They are moved by sliding up the wall as each course is laid (Figure 1.12).

A tuck jointer or brick jointer is a very useful tool for forming a recessed joint (Figure 1.13).

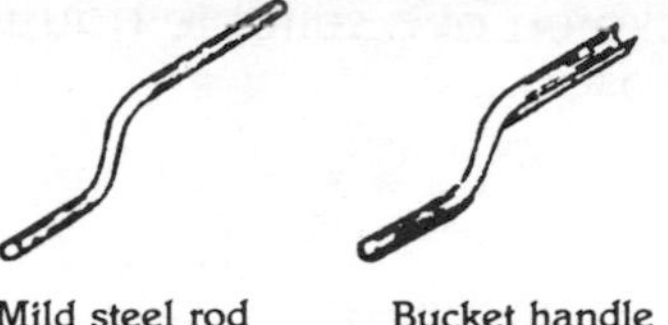

Figure 1.9 Jointing irons

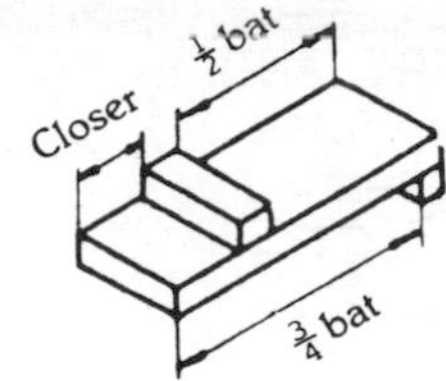

Figure 1.10 Closer gauge

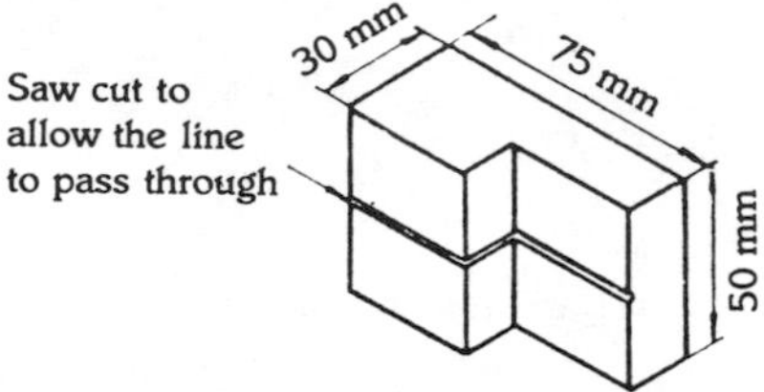

Figure 1.11 Detail of a typical corner block

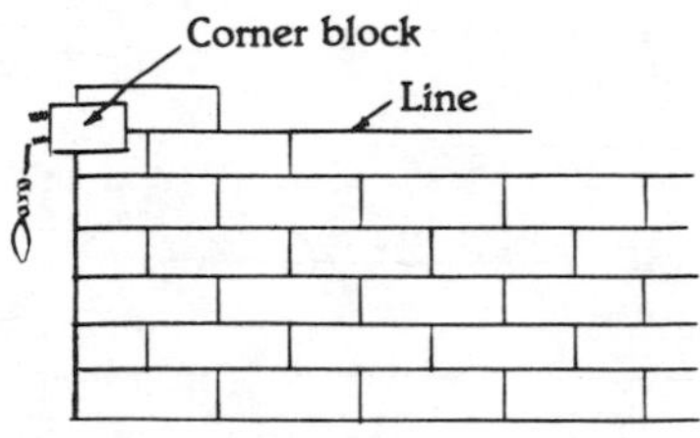

Figure 1.12 Application of a corner block

Figure 1.13 Brick jointer

Tools are usually very expensive items and should be kept clean and properly looked after. For example, at the end of each day the trowel should be thoroughly washed off and rubbed over with an oily rag, an item which should be in every tool bag. Similarly, the spirit level and line pins should be cleaned off. Tools will give many years of good service if they are well cared for.

Questions for you

5. Describe a gauge rod.

6. A gauge rod is used:
(a) to measure half bats
(b) to measure the width of door and window openings
(c) to measure the heights of courses in brickwork

a [ ]	b [ ]	c [ ]

7. Make a sketch of a suitable gauge for the marking and cutting of closers.

8. Describe two types of jointers for pointing brickwork.

____

____

____

____

Bricks

Bricks used for work which does not require any special finish, such as walling which is to be rendered or plastered, are classified as *commons.* The bricks mostly used for this type of work are *common flettons* which have no particular colour or finish. In fact, they usually have stripes across their faces where they have been stacked in the kiln and the burning has created different colours.

Facing bricks are usually well-burnt units having a constant finish to their surfaces and form a pleasing and weather-resisting walling. There are many different types of facing bricks, most having characteristics applicable to the areas in which they have been made.

The bricks which are the most popular and used more than any other type are the flettons which are machine made and comparatively easy to lay as they are square and uniform in size. These bricks are available as both *commons* and *facings.* They are basically the same brick but all the facings have one long side (the *stretcher face*) and one end (the *header face*) specially treated during manufacture.

Types of bricks

Clay bricks may be divided into classes such as:

Machine pressed bricks which have been made by pressing the clay into moulds before drying and burning. These usually have a *frog* or indentation on one or both beds of the bricks.

Wire cuts made by extruding the brick clay in the form of a long slab approximately 250 mm by 120 mm in cross section. As about 300 mm of the clay is extruded, a frame carrying a series of wires about 75 mm apart is pulled across the clay, cutting it into brick sizes. These bricks have no frogs and the beds of the bricks show the wire marks quite clearly.

Engineering bricks hard burnt bricks which are very dense. They are used for walling which is intended to carry heavy loads, and in sewers, water works, etc., where water resistance is essential.

Sand lime bricks or calcium silicate bricks are made by quite a different method from clay bricks because they are not burnt, but subjected to high pressure in a steam chamber called an *autoclave.* The bricks are made from a mixture of sand and lime with a very small amount of water added and are moulded under great pressure before being placed in the pressure chamber.

They are classified from class 1, for heavy loading, to class 4, for internal use only.

Concrete bricks are made in a similar way to sand lime bricks, except that sand and cement is used instead of sand and lime.

Moving bricks

Carrying bricks from one place to another is usually performed by a labourer. For small numbers of bricks this may be done:

- with the aid of a *hod* which is a two-sided box carried over the shoulder

- by means of a *brick lifter* which is a type of adjustable clamp. Eight or ten bricks are laid side by side, the lifter is placed over them and lifted by the handle in the middle. As the lifter is raised the bricks are clamped together, allowing them to be transported.

When bricks are delivered to the site they are usually stacked on pallets and often covered with polythene sheeting to protect them from the weather and from being stained by mud or concrete splashes. The pallets are unloaded from the lorry by means of a fork lift truck or a hydraulic fork lift crane mounted on the lorry itself. If the site is large enough to have a crane, then this may be used to transport the bricks from the central stacks to the place of working. It is important to remember that all handling of bricks is expensive so as much as possible of this work should be done by machine.

A *slicebarrow* may be used to move larger quantities of bricks. This is a type of sack truck which is used for bricks which have been delivered to the site on pallets. It is put under a banded set of bricks to transport them to the place of working.

Questions for you

9. Describe how bricks are generally classified.

____

____

10. Common bricks are those which are:
(a) used all over the country
(b) used for all of the facework on a large housing estate
(c) used for walling which is to be plastered

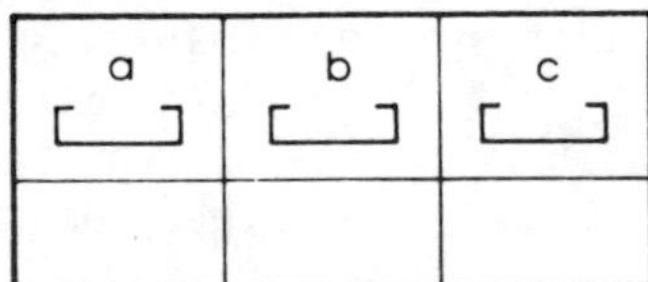

11. Sand lime bricks are made by:
(a) burning in the same way as clay bricks
(b) the sand and lime being mixed together and placed in moulds to harden
(c) subjecting them to high steam pressure in an autoclave

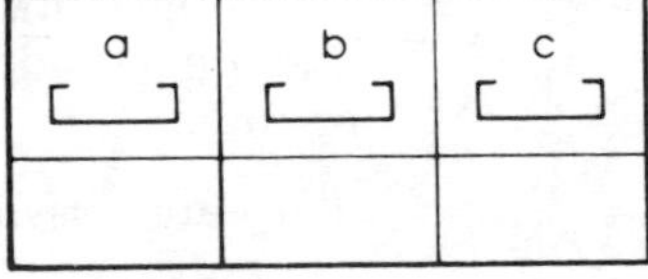

12. A brick lifter is:
(a) a fork lift truck
(b) a clamp for transporting bricks
(c) a special crane mounted on a lorry

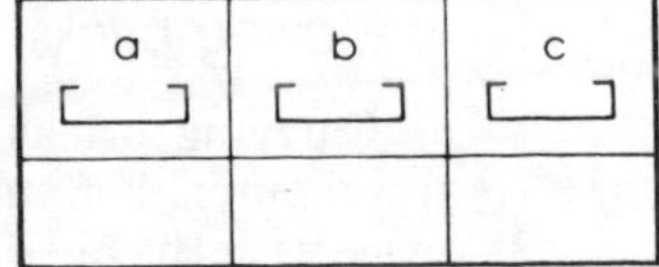

Mortars

Mortars are mixtures of either Portland cement, lime and sand (or fine aggregate), or masonry cement and sand.

Portland cement is made by burning a mixture of chalk (or limestone) and clay, which is then ground to form a very fine powder.

Masonry cement is a Portland cement to which has been added up to 25% of an air-entraining or plasticising material. This has the advantage of reducing the high strength of Portland cement, making it more suitable for general brickwork. When water is added to a mortar using masonry cement the air-entraining agent forms minute bubbles in the mix which make it very workable and easy to use. When the mortar sets these bubbles remain, making it slightly porous. This allows rainwater to evaporate and avoids the possibility of it being trapped between the bricks and freezing in severe weather, causing spalling or deterioration of the faces of the bricks.

Masonry cement is ideal for general brickwork with a mixture of one part masonry cement to three or four parts of sand. These are thoroughly mixed together in their dry state. Water is then added to give a pliable consistency commonly known as *compo* which allows for easy handling. The mortar should be mixed in its wet state for at least two minutes.

Fine aggregate or sand needs to be fine enough to pass through a 5 mm sieve. This is used to provide the bulk in the mortar.

Hydrated lime is used to provide the workability in a Portland cement/lime/sand mix.

Cement/lime/sand mortars are very good for general brickwork. For most applications a mix of 1 : 2 : 8 or 1 : 2 : 9 would be quite satisfactory. For internal work a mix of 1 : 3 : 10 could be used. Where severe conditions are likely to be encountered, such as parapet walls or boundary walls, a mix of 1 : 1 : 5 or 1 : 1 : 6 would be recommended. It is unnecessary for a mortar for general brickwork to be of great strength and in no case should it be stronger than the bricks which are bedded in it. The only requirement is for it to be strong enough to carry the weight of the walling and be resistant to frost.

Mixing mortars

The same volume of ingredients should be used in every mix. This may be done by using identical measuring boxes, one each for sand, lime and cement. They are filled to the top, emptied and the contents thoroughly mixed together in a dry state. Water is then added until the right consistency is reached. Mixing at every stage should be continued for *at least* two minutes.

For **cement/lime/sand** mixes the lime and sand may be mixed together and water added. This mixture may be kept moist by covering it with hessian or sacking until it is required for use. Then the necessary amount of cement may be added and thoroughly mixed in before sufficient water is added to make a pliable consistency.

Mixing by hand. It is important to ensure that the ingredients are thoroughly mixed together both before and after adding the water.

Mixing by machine makes the process a lot easier, but once again the dry materials should be thoroughly mixed together before adding the water. It is also important that the mixer is cleaned out at the end of the day's work. Unfortunately, as so often happens, mortar is only required at intervals. In such cases the mixer should be emptied and washed out after each mixing. If the mortar is allowed to dry inside the drum it will gradually build up a residue which will eventually create inefficient mixing and require hammering out to clean the drum.

Admixtures

Admixtures are sometimes added to mortar to:

- make it waterproof
- increase its workability
- colour it for pointing.

They are usually in the form of liquids or fine powders. The liquids can be easily added to the mortars but the powders should be kept sheltered from the wind when being added. All admixtures should be carefully measured for each mix and used strictly in accordance with the maker's instructions.

When using colouring agents for pointing mortars it is essential that the proportions of the mortar mixes are the same throughout the job in order to ensure that the finished walling will have the same colour throughout the job. Each mix, therefore, should be carefully gauged or measured and ingredients thoroughly mixed together in a dry state before the water is added. After the water is added the wet mix should be mixed again for at least two minutes.

Questions for you

13. Portland cement is made by burning a mixture of:
(a) limestone and shingle
(b) limestone and clay
(c) shingle and clay

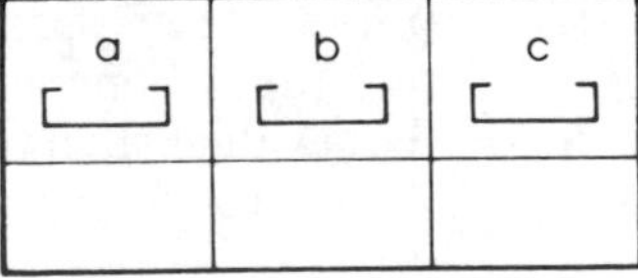

14. Mortars for general brickwork should have:
(a) the same strength as the bricks
(b) less strength
(c) greater strength

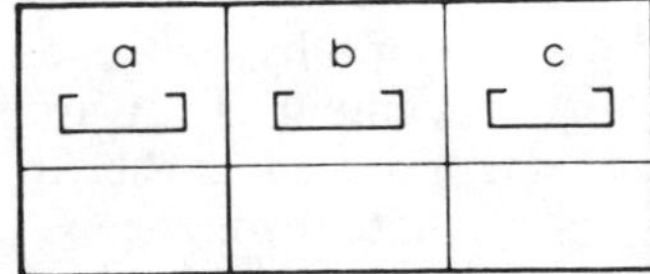

15. Describe the mix of a mortar that would be suitable for general brickwork.

Bonding

Bonding is the term given to the various recognised arrangements of brickwork in walling.

These bond patterns are essential for any wall which is intended to carry heavy loads as they prevent, as far as possible, any structural failure. For this to be effective the bonding must distribute the loading evenly throughout the length of the wall, so that each part of the wall carries a small amount of the load (Figure 1.14). If, on the other hand, the load is not distributed but localised to certain portions of the wall, then this may cause uneven settlement and cracking (Figure 1.15).

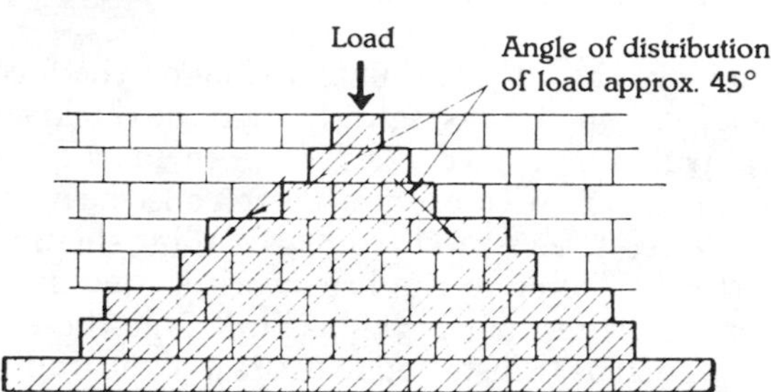

Figure 1.14 Even load distribution due to good bonding. The shaded area shows how the load is distributed over a large area of walling

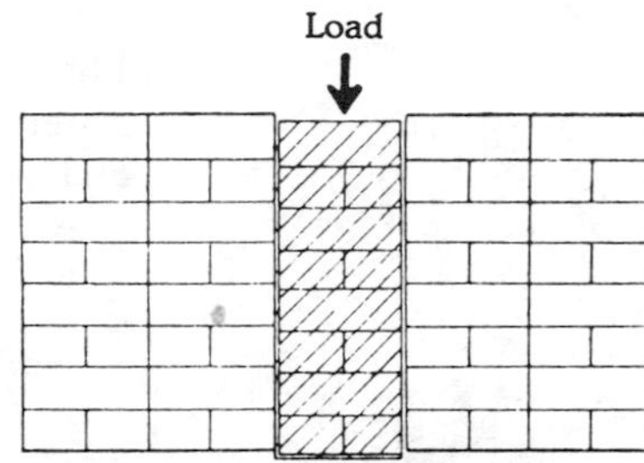

Figure 1.15 Uneven load distribution due to poor bonding. The shaded area of the walling takes all the load and has a tendency towards more settlement than the rest of the wall

The prime object of bonding, therefore, is to ensure that the walling reaches its maximum stability. This is achieved by properly bonding the bricks at all times, especially at key positions such as *quoins* or corners, junction walls and partitions. Long lengths of walling with no junction walls are liable to be quite weak along their length so it is necessary to introduce *attached piers* at intervals along the wall in order to stabilise it.

Key factors affecting the strength of brickwork are:

The slenderness ratio – the height of the walling in relation to its width. A thin wall should not be built too high as it is liable to become unstable.

The lateral strength – how long a wall may be before it is thickened by adding attached piers or buttresses. The 'length' of a wall is its total length, or the distance between two junction walls or attached piers. Thin walls can become unstable if they are built too long or are subjected to wind pressure.

The bonding of brickwork, however, is not confined wholly to strength requirements, as very often a certain bond is introduced into a wall for its pleasing appearance in addition to its strength. There are also some bonds which have little stabilising effect on the walling but are used specifically for decorative purposes. These types of bonds can be used with remarkable effect, for example, on large areas of walling which would otherwise look quite drab. They can present quite interesting architectural features which are pleasing to the eye.

In addition to strength, economy may also play an important part in the selection of a facing bond, as the number of facing bricks required will vary

according to the bond used. The table below gives the approximate number of facing bricks required per 0.84 square metre in various bonds using bricks of different depths or thickness.

Type of bond	*Thickness of brick*		
	50 mm	65 mm	70 mm
English bond	90	72	66
Flemish bond	80	64	59
English garden-wall bond	75	60	55
Flemish garden-wall bond	69	56	51
Stretcher bond	60	48	44
Header bond	120	96	88

The approximate number of facing bricks required per 0.84 m^2 of walling in various bonds

There are certain working principles which should be applied to bonding in general:

- The *perpends,* which are the vertical joints visible on the face of the wall, and the *cross joints,* which pass right through the thickness of the wall, should be kept truly vertical with each other in alternate courses.
- No perpends should coincide with each other in consecutive courses. This is commonly referred to as *straight joints.* Walling should be kept truly *plumb* or vertical. Therefore the brickwork at quoins must be correctly built, because the rest of the wall is built from these and any mistakes at the quoins will be transferred to the rest of the walling. This is explained more fully in Chapter 2, p. 17.
- The brickwork must be kept to the prescribed gauge and maintained throughout the construction of the walling. This is achieved by building the walls off a level base, or fixing levels at each of the quoins and gauging each course with the aid of a gauge rod. The gauge can be any predetermined measurement; for flettons or similar bricks a gauge of four courses to 305 mm is generally suitable (Figure 1.16).

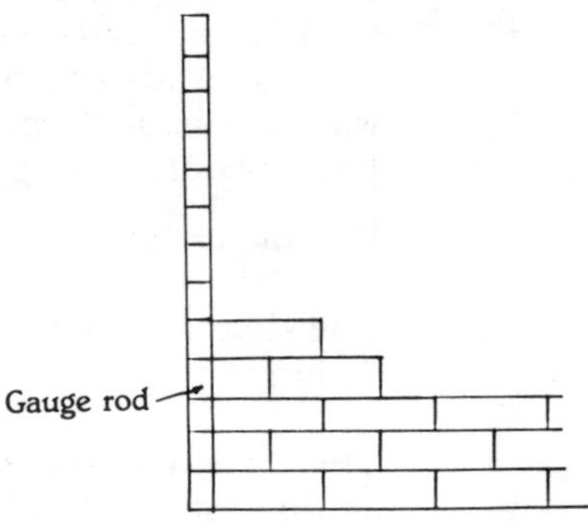

Figure 1.16 Application of a gauge rod

- The walling should be kept *level.* This means that the work must be started from a level base and the whole of the brickwork built to the same gauge. A basic level known as the *datum level* needs to be fixed. All the measurements for the building to be erected on the site can be taken from this level; see Figure 1.17. A peg is driven into the ground until the top reaches the desired height and all other levels are transferred from it. One method of transferring these levels is to use a long levelling board, as shown in Figure 1.18.
- The bricks are laid in courses and to lines which are stretched from the quoins. The top edge of each brick as it is bedded must be laid to the line; the face of the brick must also touch the line (Figure 1.19). In this way, if the quoins have been built correctly then the face of the wall will be even and the joints equal in size.

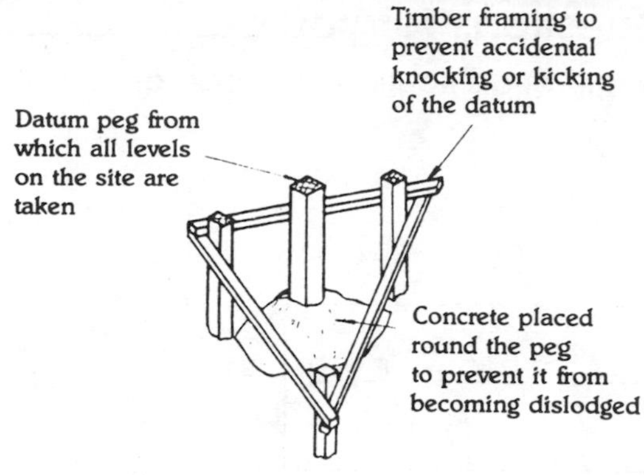

Figure 1.17 Detail of a datum peg

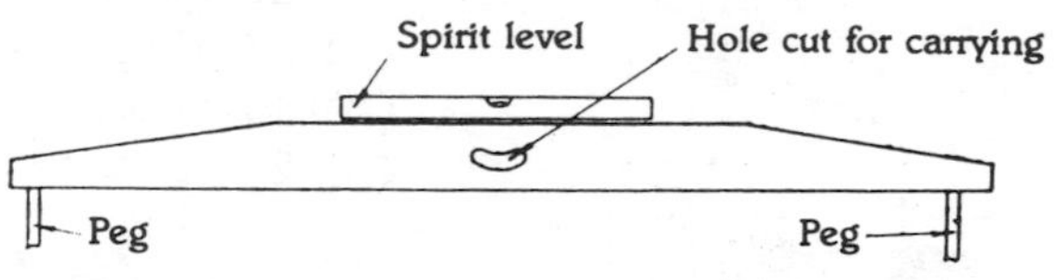

Figure 1.18 A method of transferring a level from one peg to another

- The correct *lap* should be maintained at all times. This may be done either by placing a *closer* (a unit equal to a quarter of the length of a brick) next to each quoin header, or by using a *three–quarter bat* (a unit equal to three quarters of the length of a brick) when starting each stretcher course (Figure 1.20).
- The *tie bricks,* which are the most important units bonding the walls into one another at junctions or quoins, should be well bonded to secure the walls together (Figure 1.21).
- Closers must never be built into the face of the wall other than next to the quoin header (Figure 1.22).
- The joints in the interior of the wall should be flushed in (neatly finished) at each course so that the wall is built solidly.

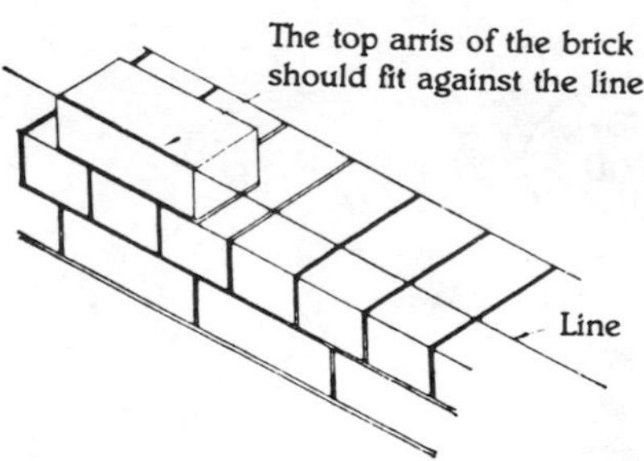

Figure 1.19 Laying a brick to a line

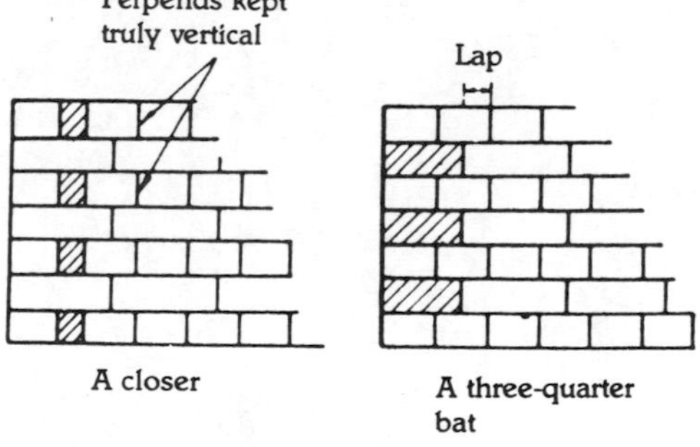

Figure 1.20 The bonds formed by a closer and a three-quarter bat

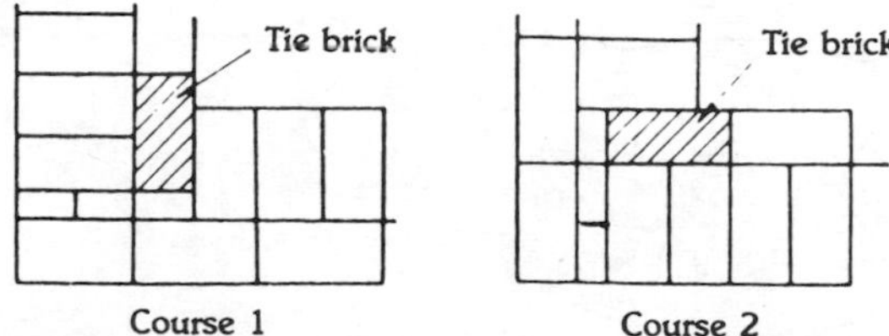

Figure 1.21 Plans showing the tie brick bonding the walls together

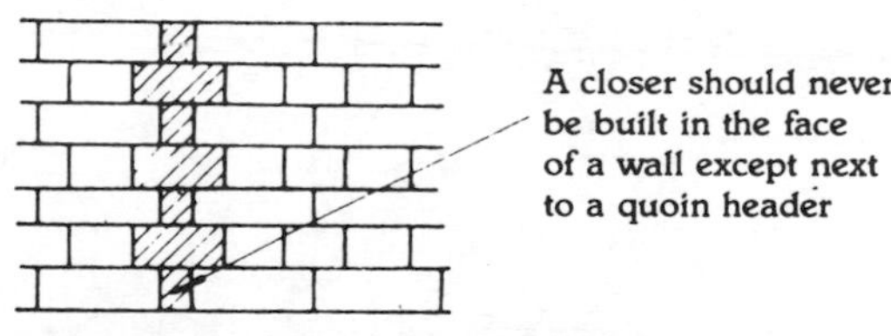

Figure 1.22 An example of bad bonding

Questions for you

16. The approximate angle of distribution of a load on a well-bonded wall should be:
(a) $67\frac{1}{2}$ degrees
(b) 45 degrees
(c) $22\frac{1}{2}$ degrees

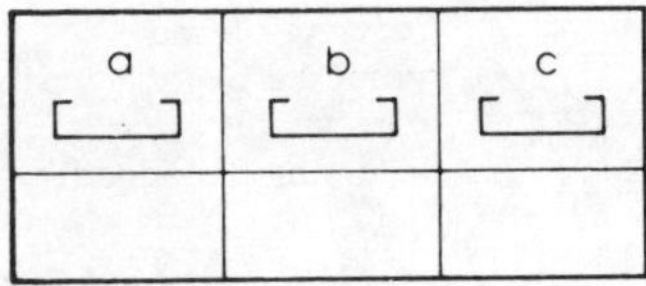

17. State what is meant by the term 'straight joint'.

18. A tie brick is:
(a) a brick used to join attached piers to the main wall
(b) a brick built in the internal angle of a quoin
(c) a brick used to join a junction wall to a main wall

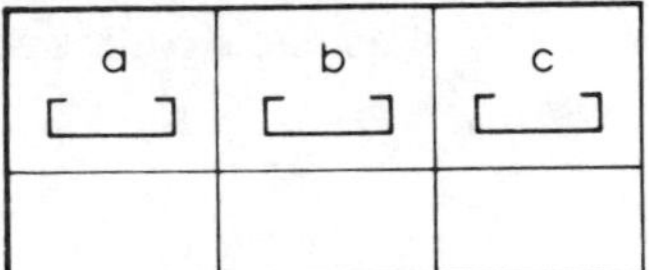

2 Solid brick walls

Methods of working

Brickwork which has been done by good craftsmen using first-class bricks has a very attractive appearance which will last for a long time. On the other hand, if the work has been carried out in a slipshod manner it will be a thoroughly bad advertisement both for the craftsman and the builder by whom he is employed, and this may well prove to have an adverse effect on the business on which both rely.

The first essentials in building are that the work should:

- be vertical.
- be truly horizontal.
- have perpends in line and truly vertical.
- have a true surface along its face.

Plumbing

For a wall to be vertical it is vital to ensure that the corners or quoins are truly perpendicular or *plumb.* As each quoin brick is laid it should be plumbed with the aid of a plumb rule and plumb-bob, or more usually in these days, with a bricklayer's spirit level (Figure 2.1). If a corner leans out, it is said to *overhang;* if it leans back, it is said to *batter.* Some craftsmen assert that it is better to build a corner with a very slight batter, but in actual practice it is far more satisfactory to keep the work truly plumb.

Levelling

The intervening bricks are laid and checked for accuracy with a straightedge

Spirit level

This brick is levelled from the quoin header and then plumbed up the face of the wall

The quoin header is levelled, gauged and plumbed

Pencil marks to indicate position of bricks to be laid

Plumbing

Left hand to hold the top, leaving the right hand free to adjust the quoin header if necessary

Foot pressed against the bottom of the spirit level

Figure 2.1 Method of plumbing and levelling a corner

Levelling

If a wall is out of level it is commonly said to *have a pig in it* and a wall like this is rather unsightly. Even if a wall has been built out of level for part of the height and then corrected by either grinding down the end which is high, that is, using very thin bed joints, or bringing up the end which is low,

it will stand out as amateurish and give the work a poor appearance. It is, therefore, necessary to keep a constant check on the work throughout its construction.

The method that is usually adopted is to fix a *peg* at each corner of the building. These are short lengths of wood about 50 by 25 by 250 mm (Figure 2.2). The tops of these pegs are carefully levelled with each other from the permanent datum peg described in Chapter 1, before the brickwork is begun. On small buildings, this may be done with the aid of a long levelling board and spirit level in a way similar to that also described in Chapter 1.

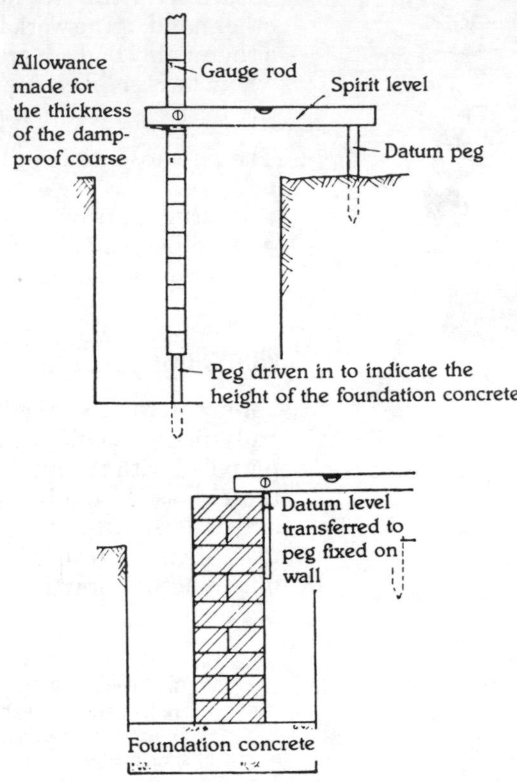

Figure 2.2 Sections showing the applications of a datum peg

Gauging

A gauge rod of 37 by 37 mm timber and of a convenient length must then be set out to show the height of the brick courses. These courses should be made to suit the thickness of the bricks plus the required thickness of joint. This is called keeping the work to gauge, and is commonly four courses to 305 mm. Alternatively it may be four courses to 325 mm or five courses to 325 mm, according to the size of bricks used. If the job is only a small one, then the courses may be pencilled on the gauge rods. If, however, the building is a large one and the gauge rods are to be in use for quite a long time, then it is a better practice to make small saw cuts at the course marks. For convenience the gauge can be used as a *storey rod,* and the length of the rod is usually at least the height of a storey so that the datum pegs can be fixed at each floor level.

Erecting a corner

When the pegs are fixed and the gauge rod set out, the corners should be erected. The corners should not be too large since it is much more economical to run a wall with the aid of a line than to build up large portions of walling in the form of corners. The corners should preferably be

racked back, as shown in Figure 2.3, since *toothing* is frowned upon by many clerks of works, because of the difficulty of ensuring a solid joint when the bricks are placed, when building up to the toothings. In such work a line of weakness could occur, and if there were any slight movement in the foundation, the defect would be quite likely to show and cause cracking.

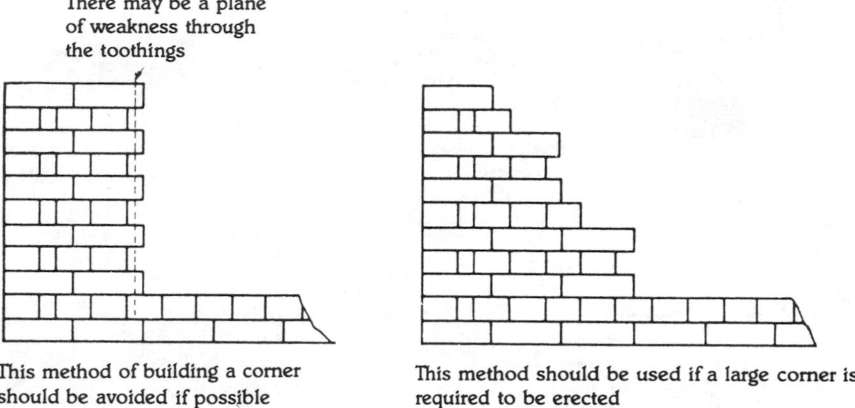

Figure 2.3 Alternative methods of corner construction

Working along the line

When the corners are built, the walling in between can be worked with the aid of either corner blocks and lines, or a line and pins. These are shown in Figure 2.4.

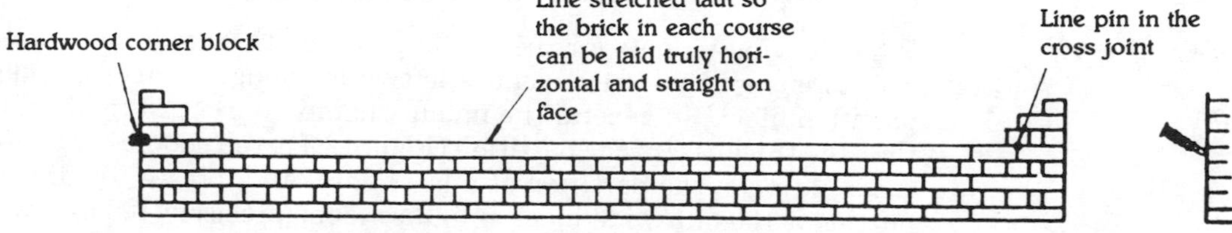

Figure 2.4 Alternative methods of supporting a line at 'the end' of a wall

Corner blocks are far more satisfactory than a line and pins, because no pin holes are made in the wall, and the pins do not get bent by being hammered into hard mortar. Once the line has been set to the length of the wall, no further adjustment is necessary, since it is simply a case of sliding the corner block up the wall to the height of each course.

Corner profiles

Instead of building corners first, an alternative method can be used in many cases, particularly with boundary walls or long walls having a plain façade. This is to erect *corner profiles,* sometimes called *dead-men profiles.* These are of planed timber fixed vertically and braced to prevent their moving, so that the line can be secured, as in Figure 2.5, without any necessity for corners. With this method the gauge can be marked on the profile and the expense of building the corner is considerably reduced. Care must be exercised to ensure that the profile is straight and fixed rigidly in an upright position.

There are also patent corner profiles on the market which serve the same purpose in a very effective way.

If the wall is a long one then the line will tend to sag in the middle. To offset this, one or more *tingles* should be provided (Figure 2.6). The height of these can be checked:

- with the gauge rod from a datum peg fixed at that point.
- by the corner-man *sighting through the line;* any discrepancy can easily be seen and corrected.

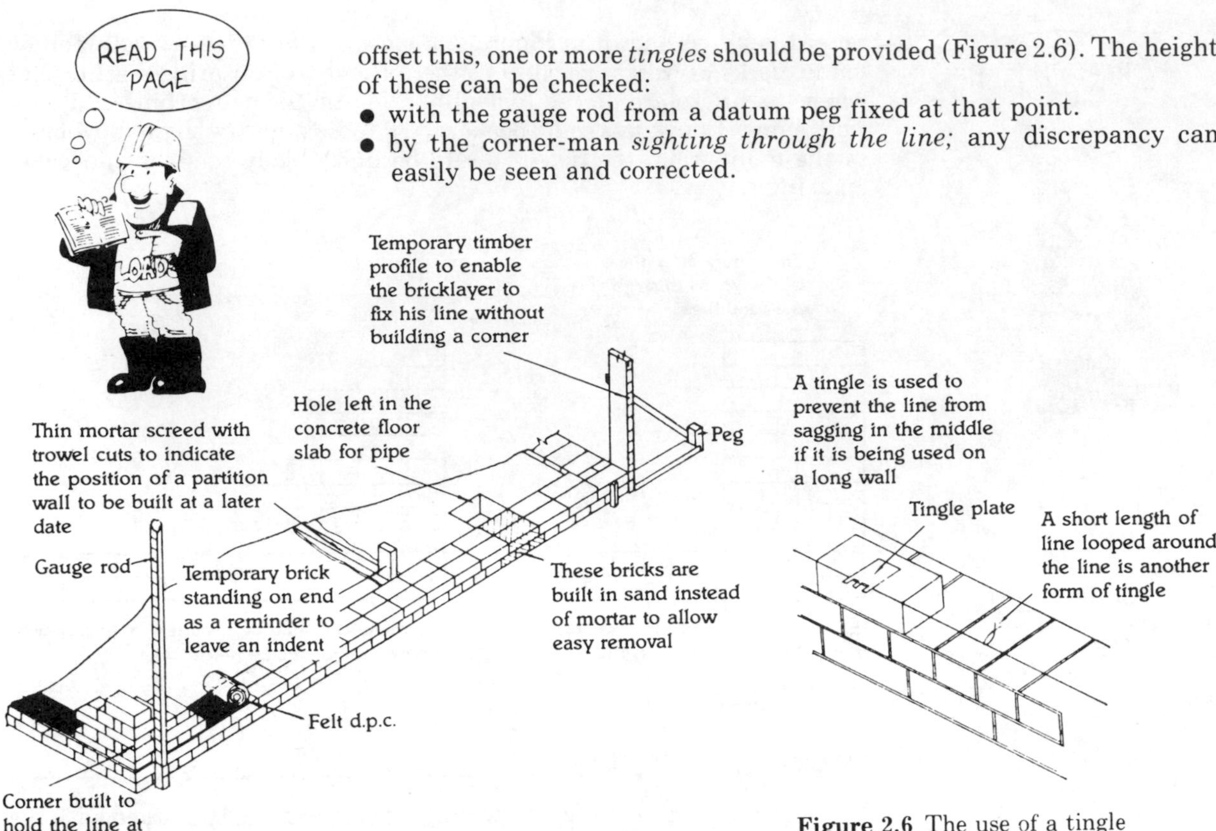

Figure 2.5 A typical setting out of an external wall for a small building

Figure 2.6 The use of a tingle

Indents and block bonding

When leaving indents for the bonding of partitions to a main wall, take care to ensure that the indent is left wide enough to accommodate the partition block. In general the indent should be from 25 to 37 mm wider than the thickness of the partition (Figure 2.7). You should try to visualise the building of the partition at a later date, and foresee the difficulty of putting a 100 mm wide block into an indent precisely 100 mm wide.

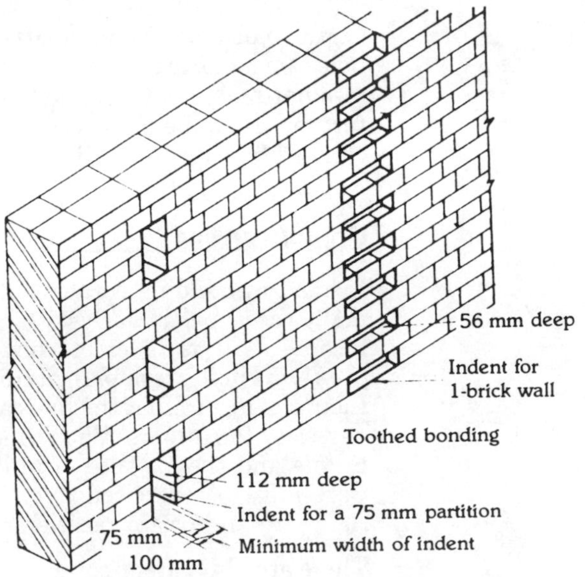

Figure 2.7 Block bonding

Clean out indents and toothings thoroughly before the wall is completed to avoid the wasteful necessity of cutting out hard mortar with a hammer and chisel when the partitions are being built. Keep the indents truly plumb. If this is not done you will need to cut away the sides of the indents with a hammer and chisel, thus causing unnecessary work and delay in building the partition.

Tolerances

Measurements in brickwork should always be reasonably accurate, but owing to the nature of the materials used it is very difficult to be precise; a certain amount of tolerance is therefore allowed as follows:

The overall height of a wall should be built to gauge ± 5 mm in 3 m height and with regular joint thickness.
The wall level should be within ± 3 mm in 2 m length.
The wall should be kept plumb within ± 3 mm in 1 m height.
The line of the facework should have no deviation more than 5 mm in 3 m length.
All perpends should be 10 mm $\pm$ 3 mm.
There should be no deviation to perpends exceeding 5 mm.

Questions for you

1. Describe a datum level.

____

____

____

____

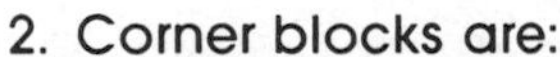

2. Corner blocks are:
(a) profiles erected at corners to avoid building the corners before the general walling
(b) temporary piers built to which to fix lines
(c) prepared pieces of wood to enable lines to be secured at corners

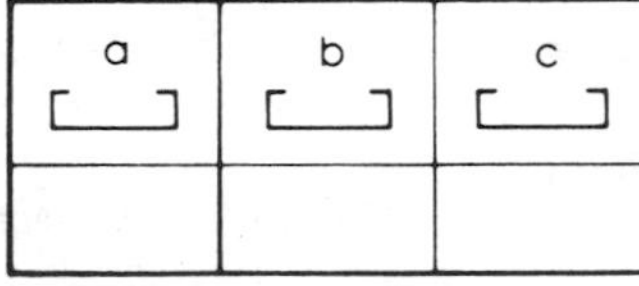

3. A tingle is:
(a) a piece of batten fixed to a wall from which the gauge rod is used
(b) a means of correcting a sag in a line
(c) a means of fixing a line to a profile

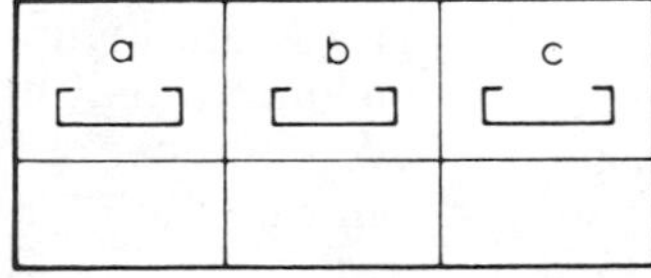

Bonds for solid brick walls

English bond

When building solid walls of one-brick thickness or more it is possible to introduce a variety of bonds consisting of headers and stretchers in different patterns. One of the commonest of these bonds is English bond, which consists of alternate courses of headers and stretchers. The bond is formed by either introducing a closer next to the quoin header or starting each stretcher course with a three-quarter bat (Figure 2.8). Both of these methods are quite acceptable but the use of the closer is the more common.

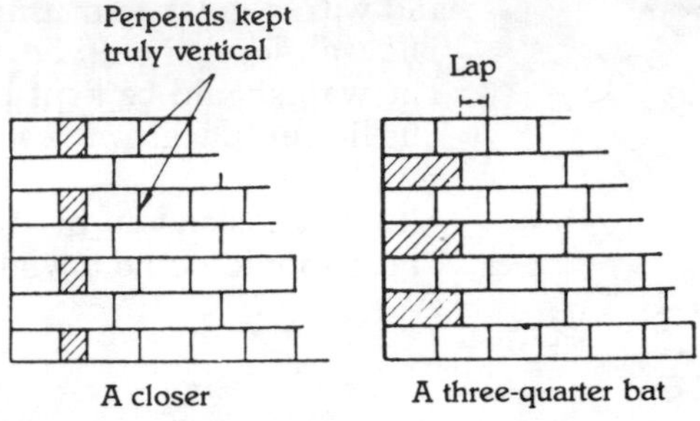

Figure 2.8 The bonds formed by a closer and a three-quarter bat

The bonding for a quoin in a one-brick wall using closers is shown in Figure 2.9. Notice that the bonding changes on the return face. The bonding for a quoin in a one-brick wall using three-quarter bats is shown in Figure 2.10. Junction walls must be tied in properly to the main wall and Figure 2.11 shows a one-brick junction wall bonded into a one-brick main wall.

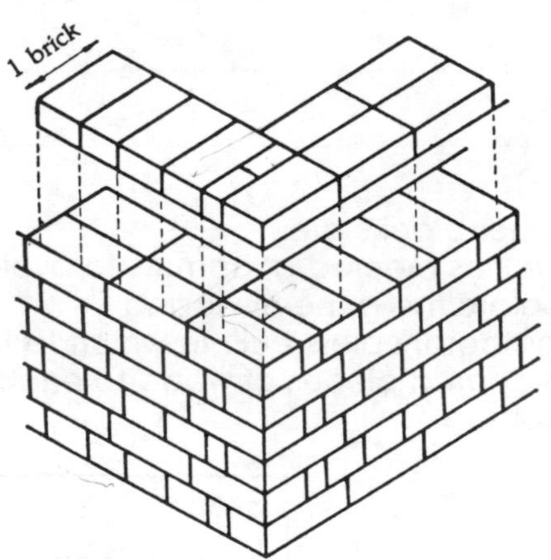

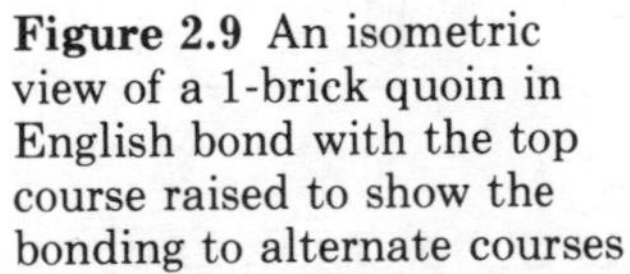

Figure 2.9 An isometric view of a 1-brick quoin in English bond with the top course raised to show the bonding to alternate courses

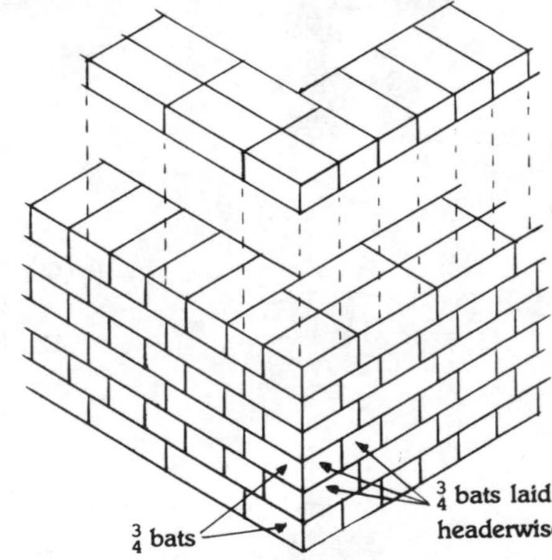

Figure 2.10 An isometric view of a 1-brick quoin built with $\frac{3}{4}$ bats in English bond

When thicker walls are being built, those having an odd number of half bricks in thickness will have opposite bonds on each course. For example, if one side has stretchers, then the opposite side will be built with headers, and so on. Figure 2.12 shows the plans of alternate courses for a quoin a one-and-a-half-brick wall built in English bond. When the walls are of an even number of half bricks in thickness, then the bond will remain the same on both faces. Figure 2.13 shows a quoin built in a two-brick thick wall.

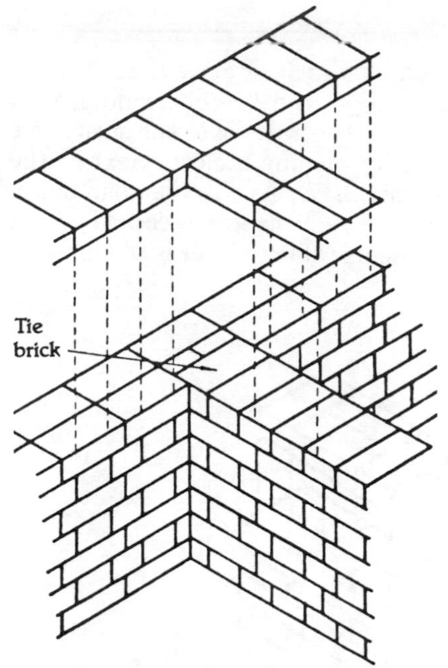

Figure 2.11 An isometric view of a 1-brick junction wall adjoining a 1-brick main wall in English bond with the top course raised to show the bonding arrangement in alternate courses

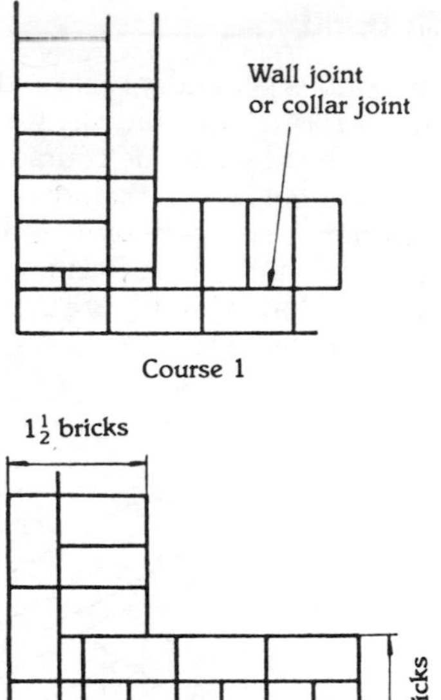

Figure 2.12 Plans showing the bonding of alternate courses of a $1\frac{1}{2}$-brick quoin in English bond

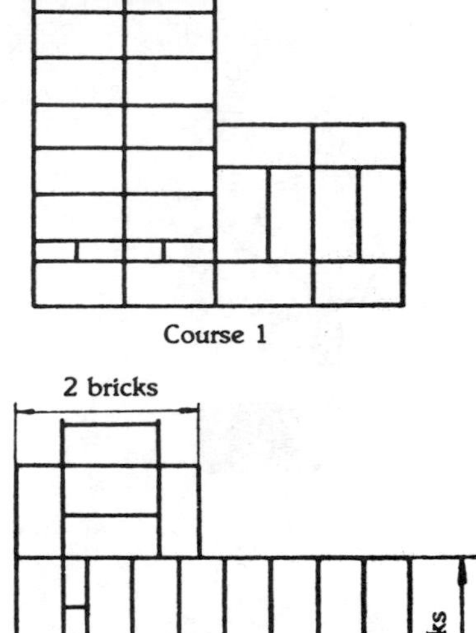

Figure 2.13 Plans showing the bonding of alternate courses of a 2-brick quoin in English bond

When bonding a junction wall to a main wall the same rules of bonding apply, in that the bond differs on the faces of one-and-a-half-brick walls. This means that the bond remains the same on *two* of the adjacent faces at the junction, i.e. stretcher course to stretcher course, and similarly with the header courses. Figure 2.14 shows this quite clearly. Figure 2.15 shows a one-and-a-half-brick wall bonded to a two-brick main wall. However, where the junction wall is an even number of half bricks in thickness the bond will change on *all* adjacent faces (Figure 2.16).

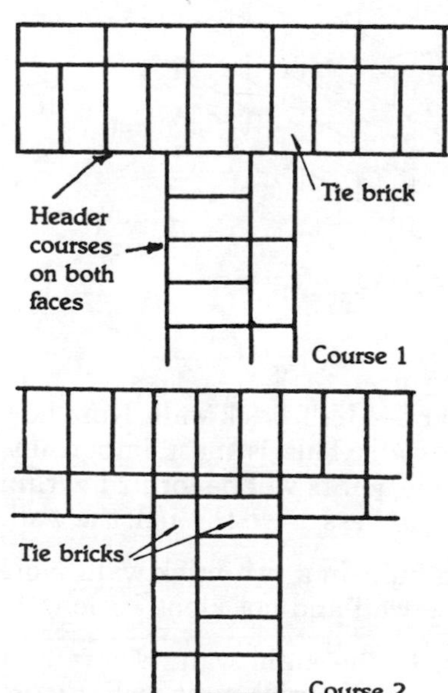

Figure 2.14 Plans showing the bonding arrangement for alternate courses in a $1\frac{1}{2}$-brick junction wall in English bond

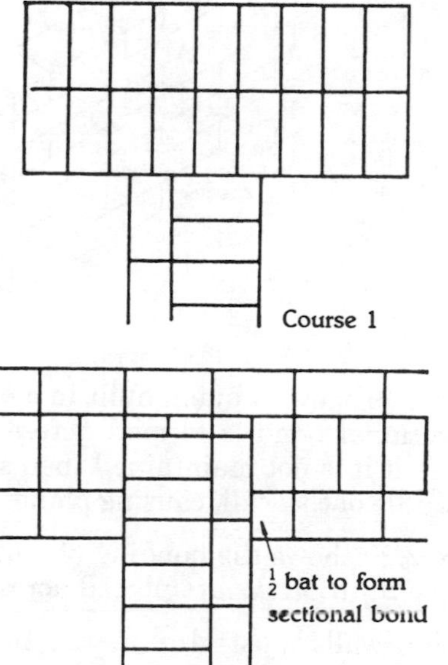

Figure 2.15 Plans of alternate courses of a $1\frac{1}{2}$-brick junction wall into a 2-brick main wall in English bond

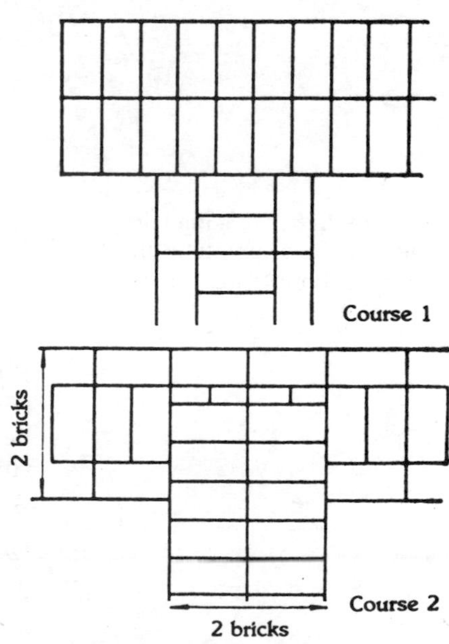

Figure 2.16 Plans showing the bonding arrangement of alternate courses for a 2-brick junction wall in English bond

Flemish bond

Flemish bond is generally regarded as being more decorative than English bond and is formed by placing alternate headers and stretchers along each course. The headers in one course are placed centrally over the stretchers in the course below. The bond is formed by placing a closer next to the quoin header or stopped-end header (Figure 2.17). As with English bond, Flemish bond can also be formed by starting each stretcher course with a three-quarter bat, as in Figure 2.18, but the use of the closer is the method more commonly used.

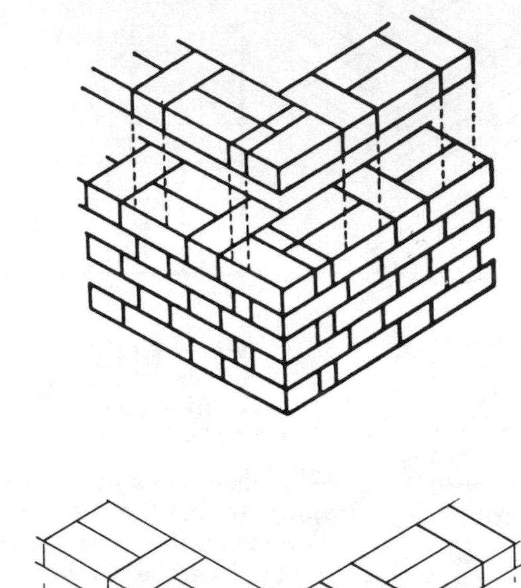

Figure 2.17 An isometric view of a 1-brick quoin in Flemish bond with the top course raised to show the bonding to alternate courses

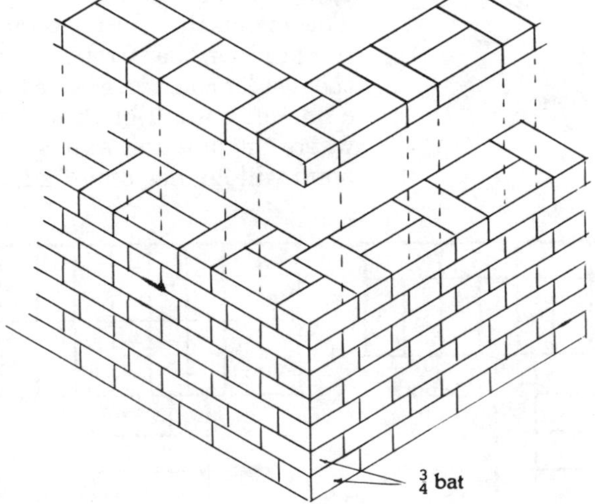

Figure 2.18 An isometric view of a 1-brick quoin in Flemish bond using $\frac{3}{4}$ bats

Figure 2.19 shows a quoin built in a one-and-a-half-brick wall. Note how the sectional bond is formed across the wall. This is most important, because if it is not maintained then straight joints will be formed within the middle of the wall, causing planes of weakness down through the wall.

Figure 2.20 shows the bonding of a quoin built in a two-brick wall. Note that the *infill bricks* are placed across the wall and not along its length.

Junction walls must also be well tied-in to the main wall; Figure 2.21 shows a one-brick junction wall bonded into a one-brick main wall. Figure 2.22 shows a one-and-a-half-brick junction wall bonded into a one-and-a-half-brick main wall. Figure 2.23 shows a two-brick junction wall bonded into a two-brick main wall, and Figure 2.24, a one-and-a-half-brick junction wall into a two-brick main wall. Note that in all cases the junction walls are bonded right across the main wall as far as possible.

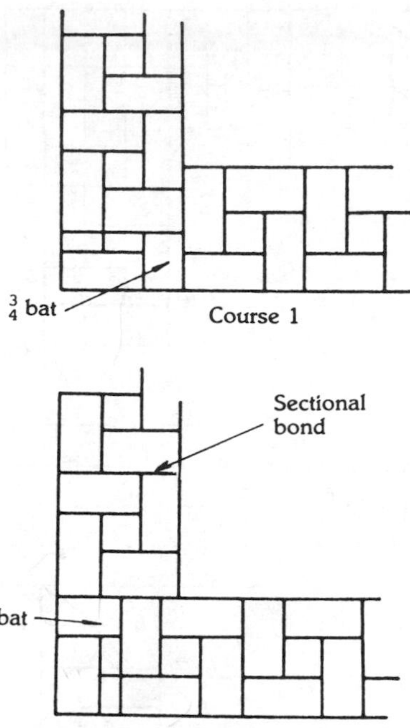

Figure 2.19 Plans showing the bonding of alternate courses of a $1\frac{1}{2}$-brick quoin in Flemish bond

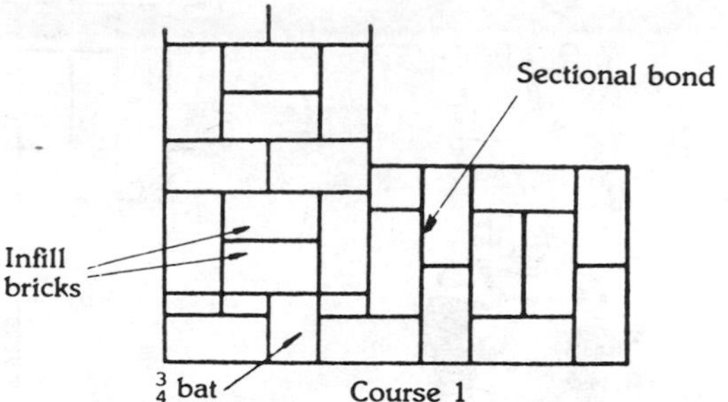

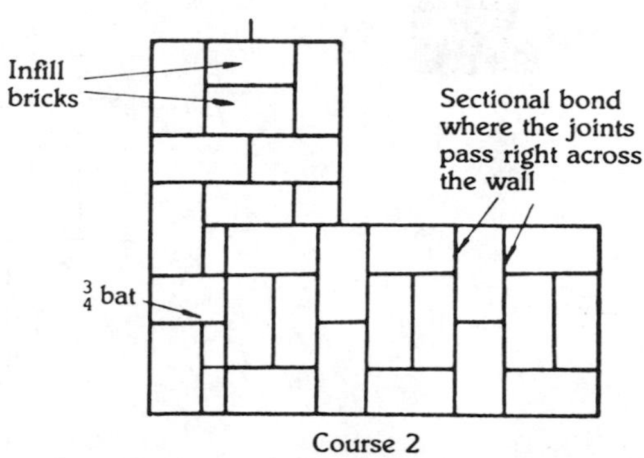

Figure 2.20 Plans showing the bonding of alternate courses of a 2-brick quoin in Flemish bond

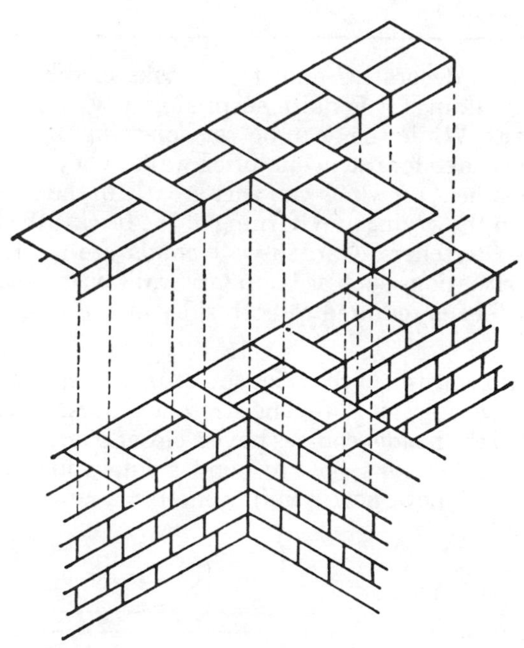

Figure 2.21 An isometric view of a 1-brick junction wall adjoining a 1-brick wall in Flemish bond, with the top course raised to show the bonding arrangements in alternate courses

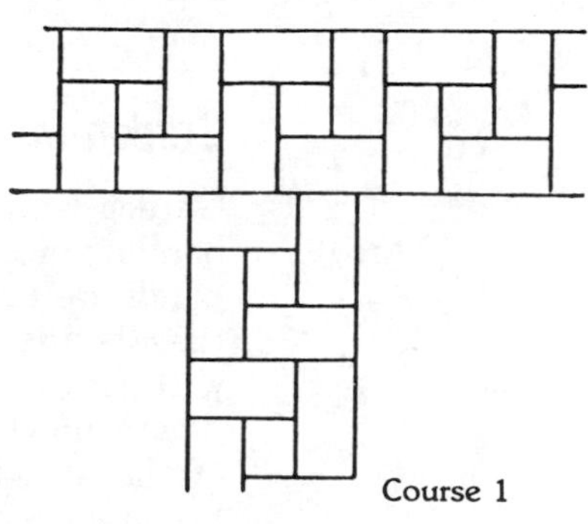

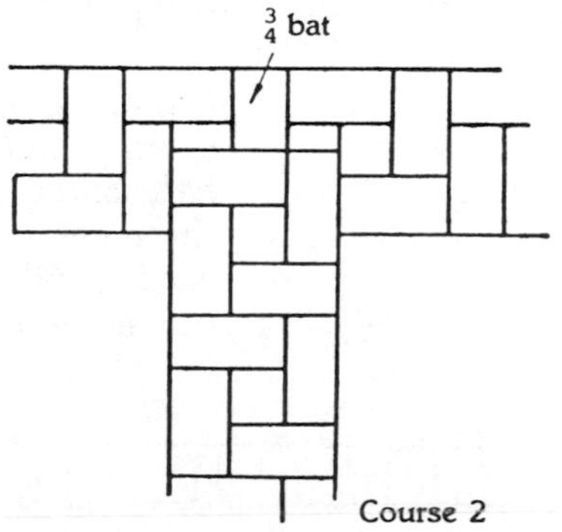

Figure 2.22 Plans showing the bonding arrangement for alternate courses in a $1\frac{1}{2}$-brick junction wall in Flemish bond

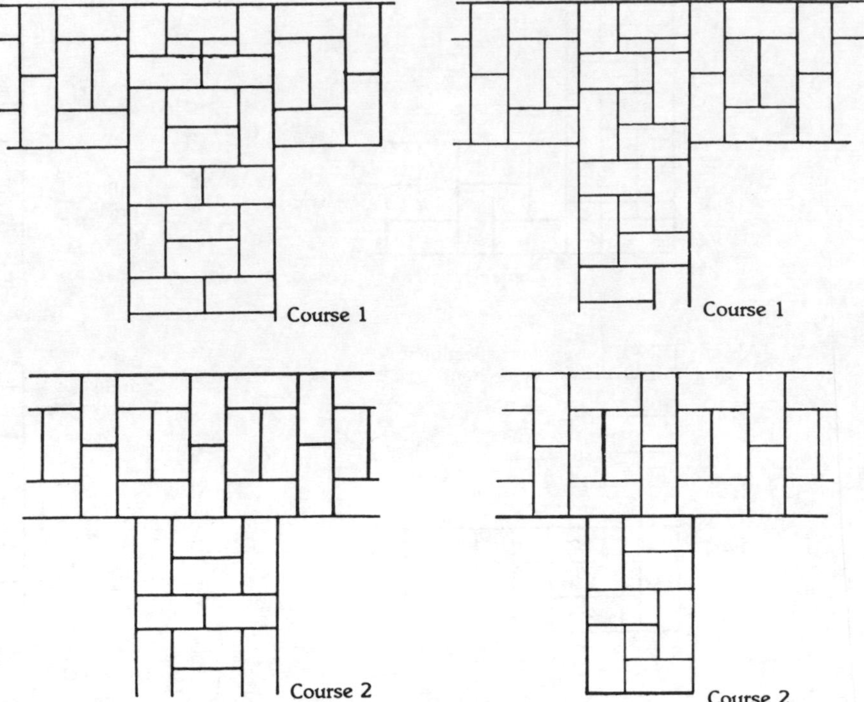

Figure 2.23 Plans showing the bonding arrangement for alternate courses in a 2-brick junction wall in Flemish bond

Figure 2.24 Plans of alternate courses of a $1\frac{1}{2}$-brick junction wall into a 2-brick main wall in Flemish bond

Garden-wall bonds

Garden-wall bonds are very decorative and if one looks closely at the bonding of brickwork in buildings it is quite surprising how often these bonds are used in facework. While they can be very pleasing to look at, these bonds are mainly intended for use in one-brick walls. They are built with a minimum number of headers which can vary greatly in their length due to uneven shrinkage in the drying and burning of the bricks; the bulk of the wall is built with stretchers. Garden-wall bonds are so named because they are used in situations such as boundary walls or to separate two gardens where a fair face is required to both sides of the wall.

English garden-wall bond consists of three, or sometimes five, stretcher courses to one header course (Figure 2.25). The stretcher courses are laid half bond to each other and the header courses have a closer placed next to the quoin header. Figure 2.26 shows how to bond a quoin in English garden-wall bond. Figure 2.27 shows how to built a one-brick junction wall into a one-brick main wall.

Using three stretcher courses to one header course

Using five stretcher courses to one header course

Figure 2.25 English garden-wall bonds

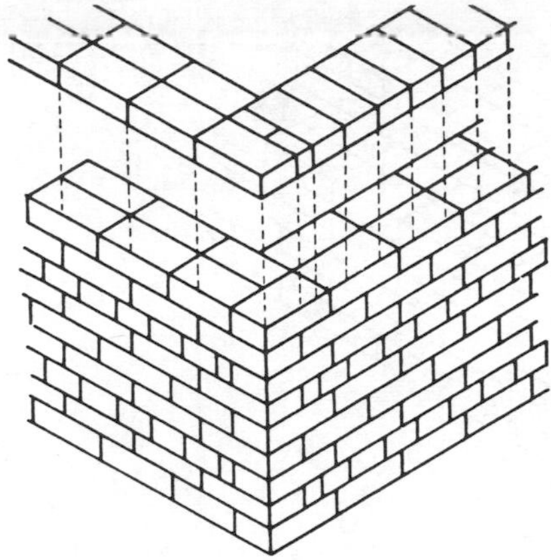

Figure 2.26 An isometric view of a 1-brick quoin in English garden-wall bond with the bond raised to show the bonding to alternate courses

Figure 2.27 Bonding of a 1-brick junction wall into a 1-brick main wall in English garden-wall bond.

Flemish garden-wall bond is an excellent bond for boundary walls and consists of three, or sometimes five, stretchers to each header in every course. The header is laid centrally over the middle stretcher in the course immediately below it, as shown in Figure 2.28. Figure 2.29 shows the bonding arrangement for a quoin. Figure 2.30 illustrates the bonding for a junction wall.

Using three stretchers to one header

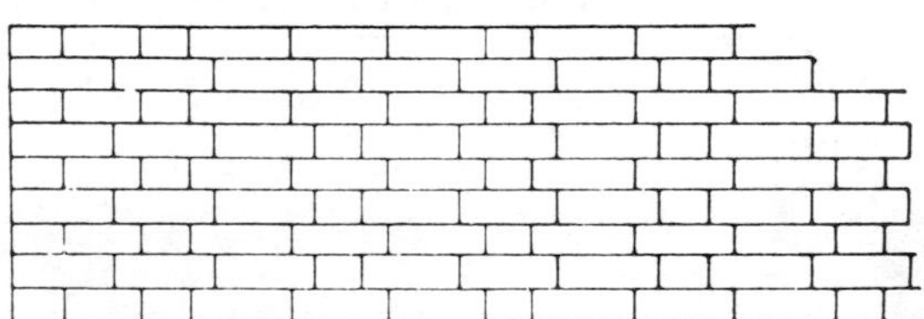

Bonding from the quoin

Using five stretchers to one header

Figure 2.28 Flemish garden-wall bonds

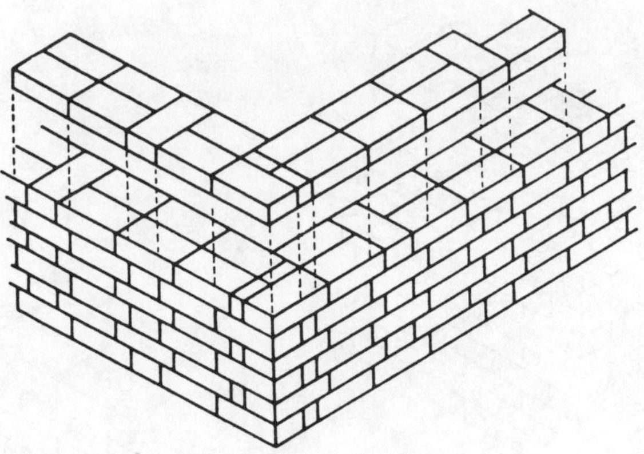

Figure 2.29 An isometric view of a 1-brick quoin in Flemish garden-wall bond with the top course raised to show the bonding to alternate courses

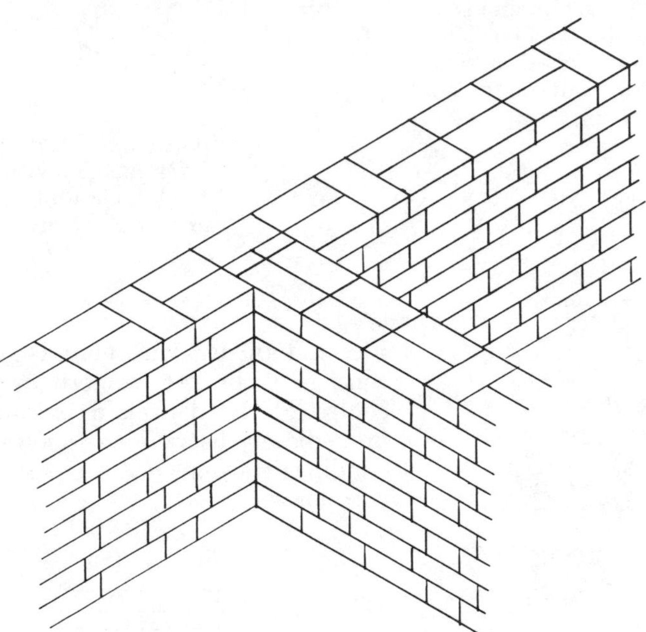

Figure 2.30 Bonding of a junction wall in Flemish garden-wall bond

Questions for you

4. Draw **TWO** elevations of a wall built in English bond showing alternate methods of bonding from a stopped end.

5. Draw plans showing the bonding of alternate courses of a one-and-a-half brick junction wall with a two-brick main wall in English bond.

6. Describe, with the aid of a sketch, the pattern of Flemish bond.

7. Describe **TWO** methods of bonding with English garden-wall bond.

8. Describe **TWO** methods of bonding a wall in Flemish garden-wall bond.

Setting out

When setting out walling on the site of a new building, *profiles* should be erected in such a way that they are well clear of the trenches. This allows the trenches to be dug without interfering with the lines. Each profile should show quite clearly the exact widths of the trench and the wall, as shown in Figure 2.31.

An alternative method of fixing a corner profile is shown in Figure 2.32.

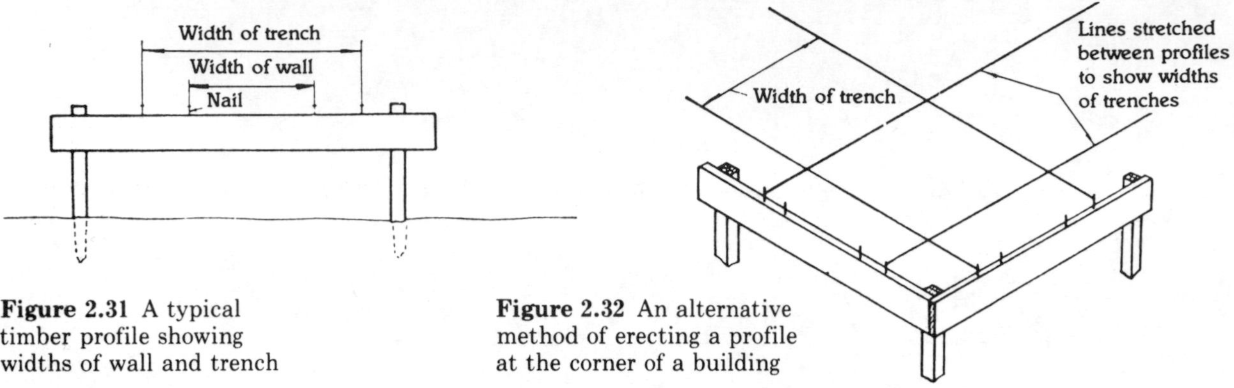

Figure 2.31 A typical timber profile showing widths of wall and trench

Figure 2.32 An alternative method of erecting a profile at the corner of a building

Setting out the base of the wall

When transferring the line of walling from the building line a thin screed of mortar is first spread on the top of the concrete foundation, then the wall line is transferred from the building line stretched between the profiles by means of a spirit level. The wall line is marked in the mortar screed by means of the trowel, as shown in Figure 2.33.

Figure 2.33 Setting out the base of the wall

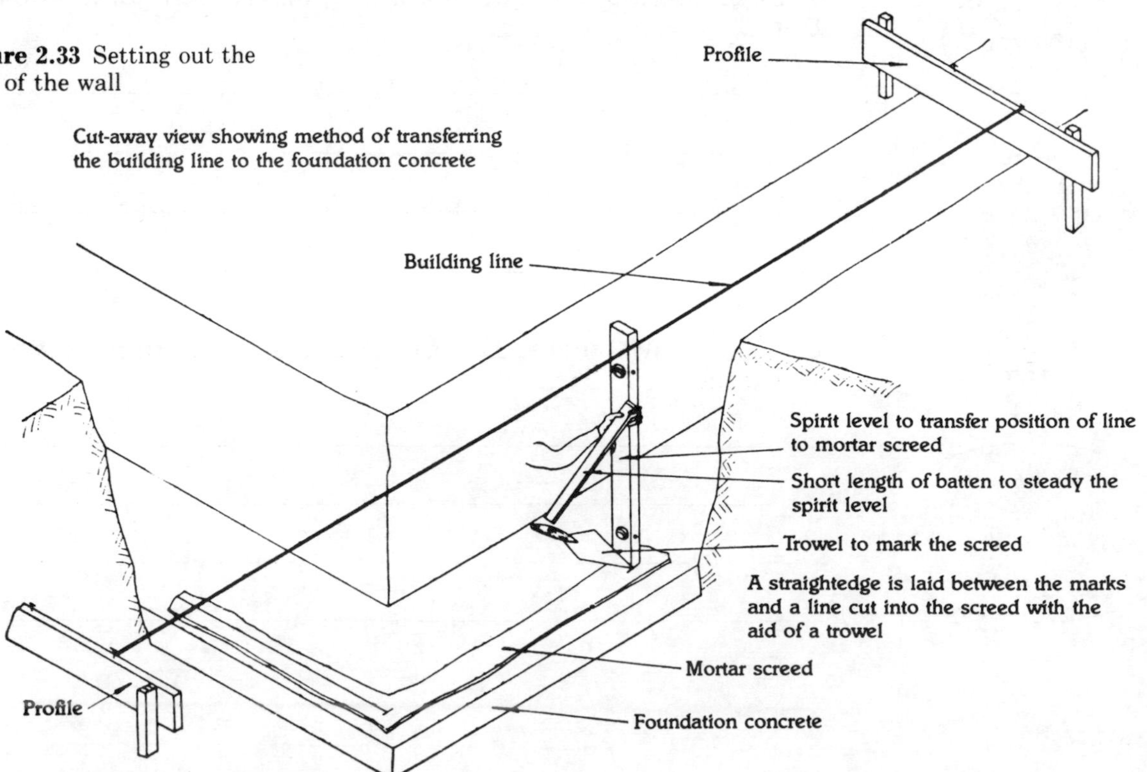

Questions for you

9. A profile, when applied to setting out, is:
(a) a point from where levels are taken
(b) a length of board cut to show the shape of a wall curved on plan
(c) a framework to which to fix lines

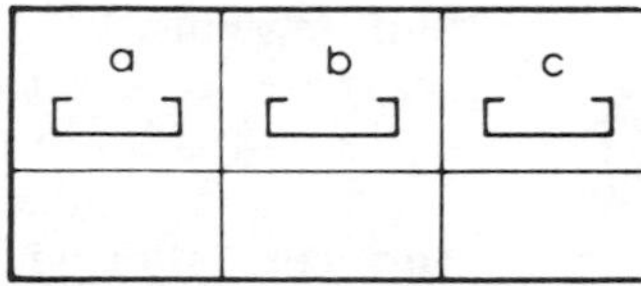

10. Explain how profiles are used for setting out walling.

11. Describe how to transfer the building line to the foundation base.

Damp-proofing

Oversite concrete

The Building Regulations require that the whole of an area under a building must be covered with a layer of concrete, known as the *oversite concrete*. This must be provided to prevent rising damp from the ground entering the building and also to exclude the growth of plant life underneath the floor. The oversite concrete is usually laid on a layer of *hardcore*. Hardcore is formed of broken brick or stone which provides a hard level base on which to lay the concrete. It must be clean and should not contain water soluble sulphates which may cause damage to the concrete.

Damp-proof courses

The Building Regulations require that no wall or pier must permit the passage of moisture from the ground to the inner surface or to any part of the building that would be harmfully affected by such moisture. Therefore, a damp-proof course (d.p.c.) must be provided at a height of not less than 150 mm above the ground level adjoining the wall. The types of materials that would be very suitable for damp-proof courses would include the following:

- Reinforced plastic sheeting.
- A layer of bituminous felt.
- Bituminous felt with a very thin layer of lead in the middle.
- A layer of pitch polymer felt.
- Two or more courses of engineering bricks laid in English bond in Portland cement mortar 1 : 3.
- Two courses of slate laid half-bond in Portland cement mortar 1 : 3.
- Asphalt in one or two layers laid hot across the wall.
- A layer of non-ferrous metal such as sheet lead, copper or zinc.
- A layer of waterproofed cement mortar.

All walls, including sleeper walls, must be provided with a d.p.c. to safeguard them and the floors from becoming wet through rising damp. In timber floors the damp-proof course must be laid immediately below the lowest timber member, but in solid floors the d.p.c. is laid at the same level as the upper surface of the floor (Figure 2.34).

Figure 2.34 1-brick external walls showing hollow and solid floor construction

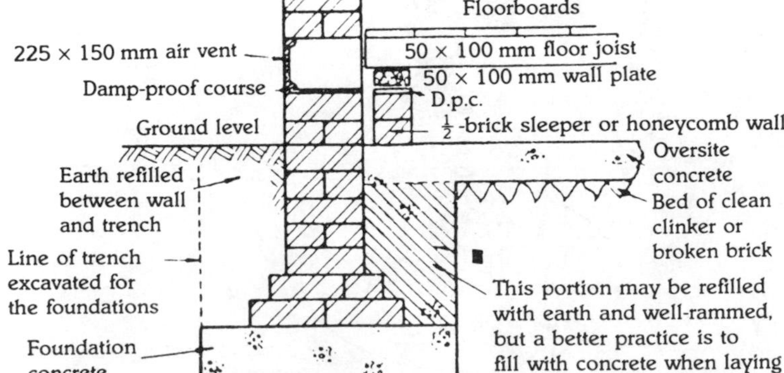

Section through a 1-brick external wall showing a solid floor construction

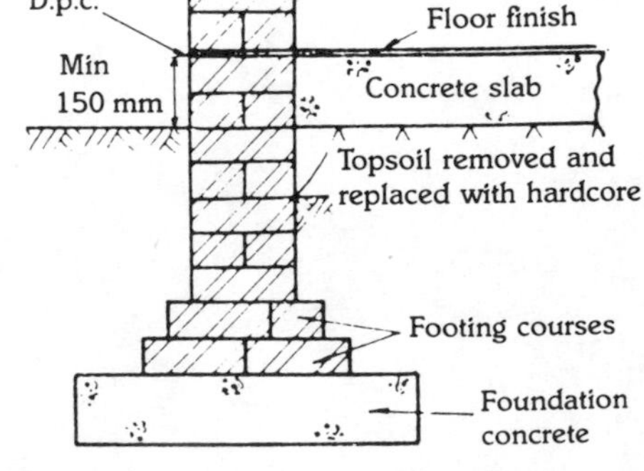

Section through a 1-brick external wall showing a hollow floor construction

Laying damp-proof courses. Bituminous felts and pitch polymer felts are similar in appearance and are used in the same way. The bituminous felts are bitumen-based while the pitch polymer felts are pitch-based. The polymer stabilises the pitch and makes it strong enough to take the weight of the walling.

Where the d.p.c.s overlap either at junctions or at the end of the roll, the minimum lap should be 100 mm. It is sometimes recommended that where lapping occurs a sealing agent is painted on the surface to ensure that the sheets are thoroughly joined together. It is also good practice for all the damp-proof course to overlap the face of the wall by 2 mm in order to prevent dampness creeping past the d.p.c. to the facework above.

All the felts should be laid on a very thin layer of mortar in order to provide an even surface. Care should be taken to ensure that there are no stones in this mortar, otherwise there is always a possibility that when the walling is built above the d.p.c. the weight of the walling might puncture the felt. Similarly when laying the first course of bricks above the d.p.c. there should be no stones in the mortar, again to avoid any damage being done.

Walling below ground level

Because of the cost of the bricks and their laying it is often more economical to build the walling below ground level with concrete blocks. It is usual to start the facework about two courses below ground level to allow for fluctuations in the finished groundwork. It is essential that the blockwork should not be visible when the building is completed and the ground level has been made up to the finished height.

On sloping sites the blocks would have to be stepped according to the slope of the ground. Similarly, the d.p.c. would also have to be stepped according to the slope of the ground. In this case, the lowest points of the d.p.c.s would have to be not less than 150 mm above the ground level, as shown in Figure 2.35.

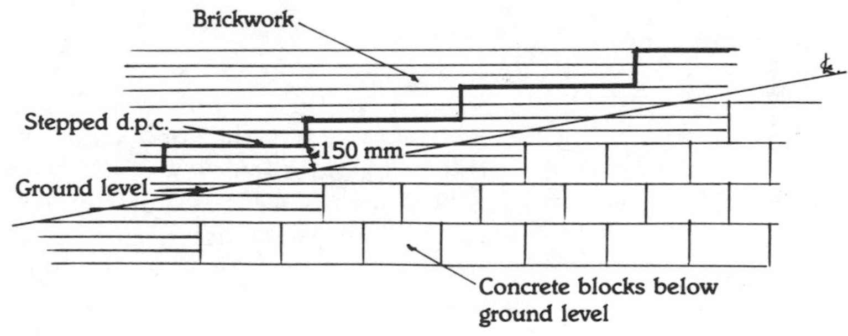

Figure 2.35 Stepped damp-proof course

Ventilation

If air circulates quite freely underneath a floor, it will absorb any free moisture, thus preventing the humid condition which encourages the growth of dry rot. To enable the air to reach the underfloor space, air vents are built at frequent intervals around the base of the building, as shown in Figure 2.34. The sizes of these vents may be 225 by 75 mm, 225 by 150 mm or, 225 by 225 mm. The larger sizes are more efficient because they allow more air to enter the underfloor space. Other forms of ventilation make use of *airbricks.* Their use is described in detail in *Brickwork 2.* It is good practice to build in ventilators on opposite walls so that draughts of air are created which pass right across the underfloor space. These ventilators may be bridged by using a slate as shown in Figure 2.36 or Welsh arch as shown in Figure 2.37.

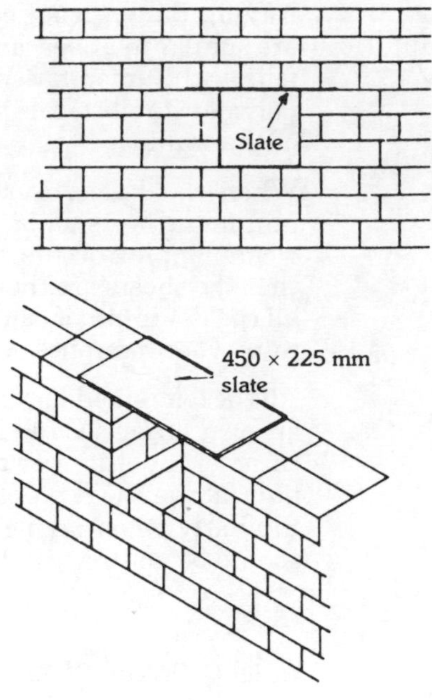

Figure 2.36 Bridging a small opening by means of a slate

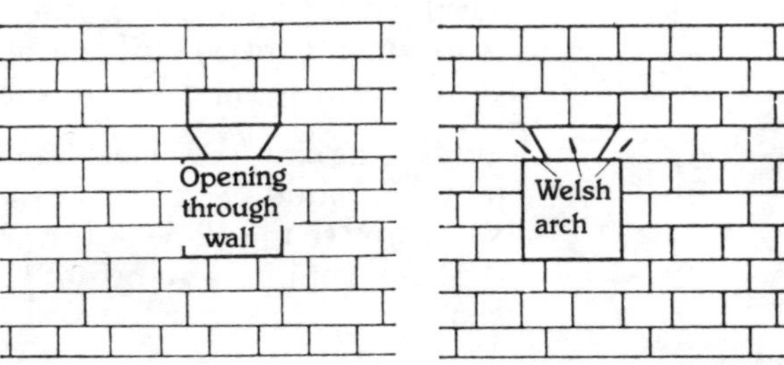

Figure 2.37 Alternative methods of building a Welsh arch

Sleeper walls are hollow or honeycomb walls built off the oversite concrete to carry the timber flooring. They are built with gaps through them to allow a free flow of air underneath the floor, as shown in Figure 2.38. A *wall plate* is laid on top of the sleeper wall to receive the timber joists. Wall plates are lengths of timber usually 100 mm × 775 mm. A d.p.c. must be laid between the top of the sleeper wall and the wall plate.

Figure 2.38 Alternative methods of building 112 mm honeycomb or sleeper walls

Questions for you

12. State the reason why damp-proof courses are placed in the walls of a building.

____

____

13. State the minimum height that a d.p.c. should be placed above the ground in an external wall.

____

14. Describe the particular care that must be taken when laying a d.p.c.

____

____

15. A wall plate is:
(a) a length of timber on which the joists rest
(b) a length of timber for checking that the wall is straight along its face
(c) a length of timber for checking that each course is laid evenly

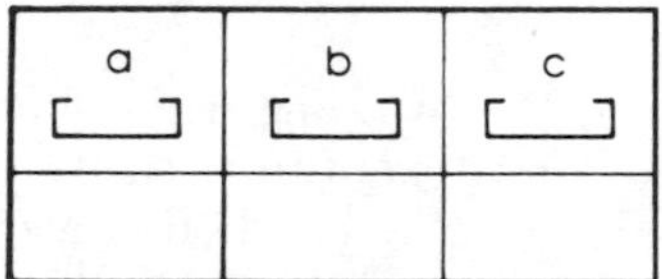

a	b	c

Copings

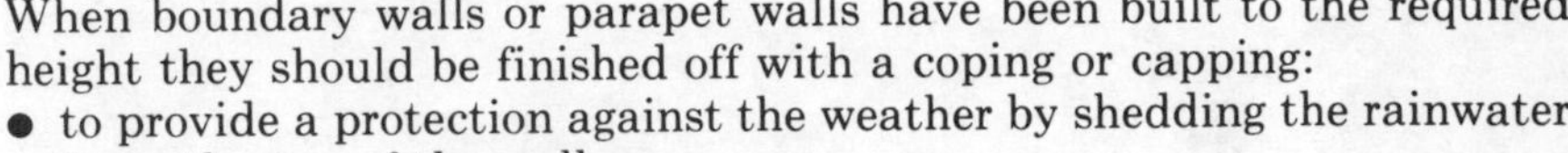

When boundary walls or parapet walls have been built to the required height they should be finished off with a coping or capping:

- to provide a protection against the weather by shedding the rainwater from the top of the wall.
- to give a decorative finish to the top of the wall.

Copings may be formed from natural stone or stone-faced concrete. The most common shapes are saddle back, shown in Figure 2.39, and feather edge, shown in Figure 2.40.

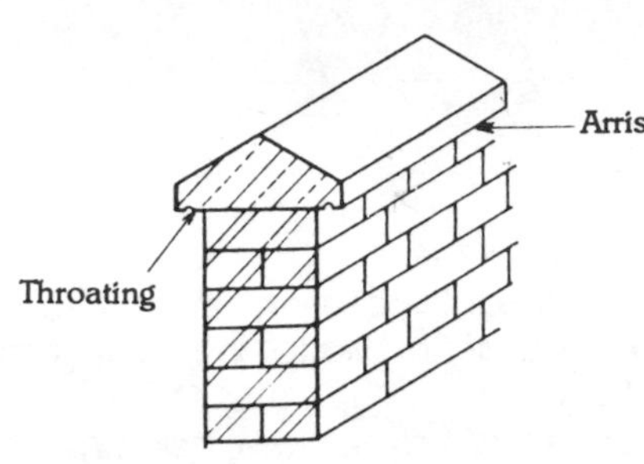

Figure 2.39 A stone saddle-back coping

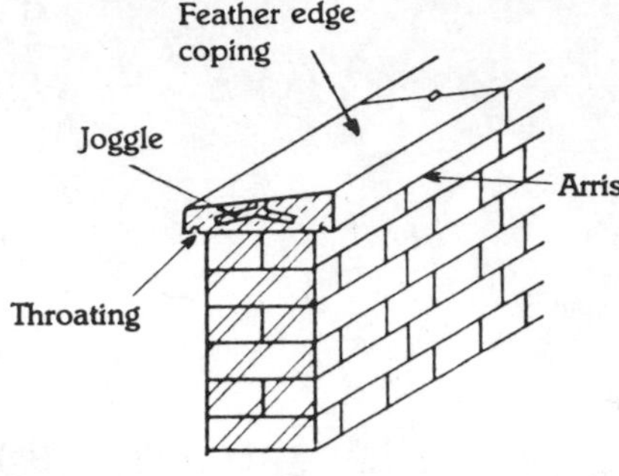

Figure 2.40 Feather-edged coping

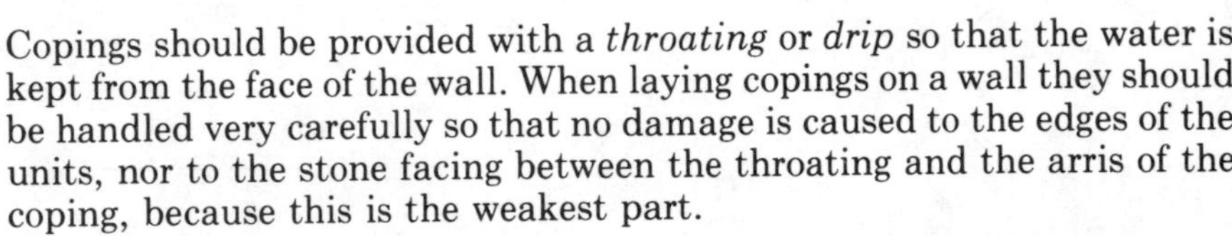

Copings should be provided with a *throating* or *drip* so that the water is kept from the face of the wall. When laying copings on a wall they should be handled very carefully so that no damage is caused to the edges of the units, nor to the stone facing between the throating and the arris of the coping, because this is the weakest part.

Coping stones may be secured by joggle joints, as shown in Figure 2.40. These are grouted in after the stones are laid with a white cement grout through a small hole at the top of the stone. This grout may be left about 25 mm from the surface of the stone. Sometimes this recess is then pointed with a mix of stone dust and white cement to match the texture of the coping stone.

Tolerances
Concrete copings should be laid level to within ± 5 mm in a 3 m length. The joints should be regular in size to within ± 3 mm and should have a uniform finish.
The copings should have uniform projection on each side of the wall.

Purpose-made bricks may also be used to cap a wall and a typical finish is shown using coping bricks in Figure 2.41 and half round bricks in Figure 2.42. Other common types of capping are brick-on-edge and brick-on-edge with tile creasing.

Brick-on-edge capping is shown in Figures 2.43 and 2.44. This is laid on the top of the wall, preferably with a slight slope to throw off any rain water which may otherwise tend to collect on the top of the wall. If the bricks are laid from each end of the wall the brick courses should be set out with the aid of a measuring tape or gauge rod used horizontally in order to avoid having a cut brick in the middle of the wall. It is most important to remember to allow for an extra bed joint for the last brick to be laid. If the

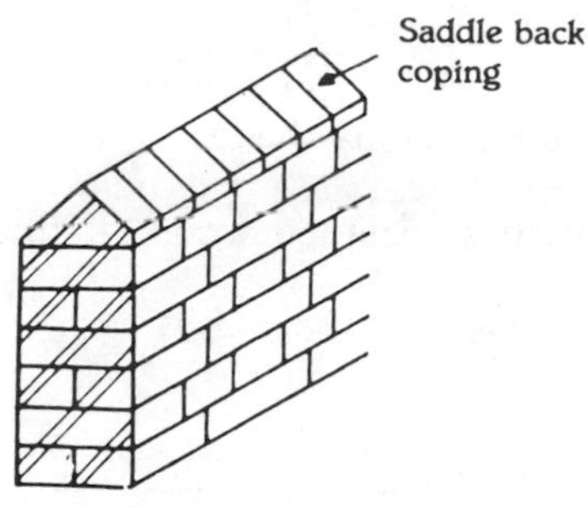

Figure 2.41 Saddle-back coping using purpose-made bricks

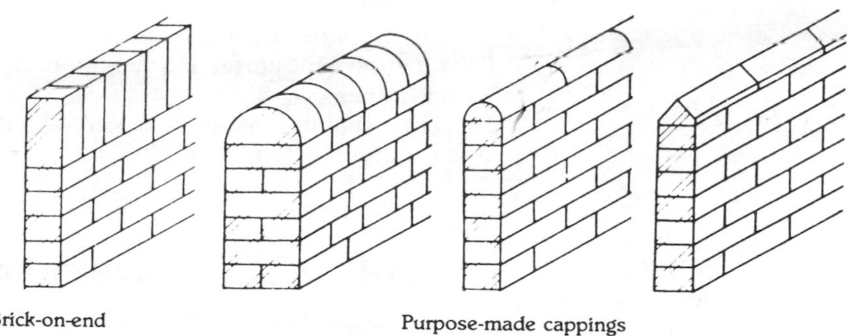

Figure 2.42 Suitable cappings for boundary walls

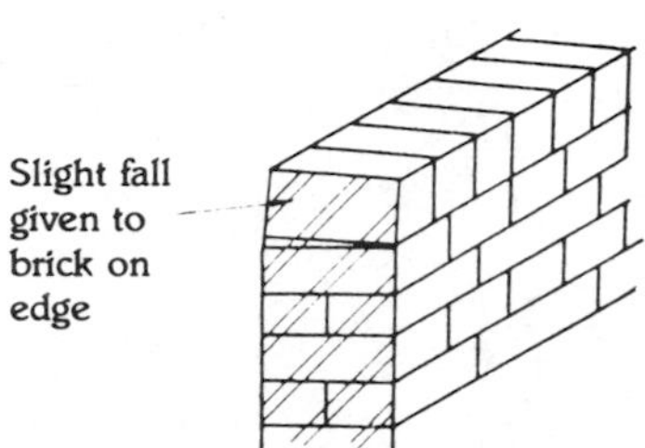

Figure 2.43 Brick-on-edge capping

Figure 2.44 Bonded brick-on-edge capping for a $1\frac{1}{2}$-brick wall

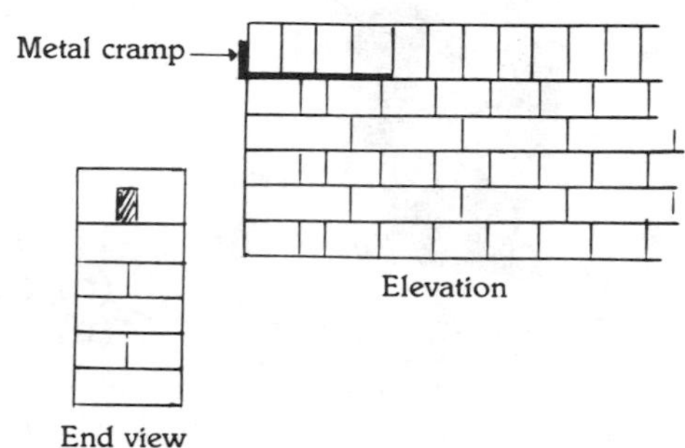

Figure 2.45 Brick-on-edge capping with metal cramp

bricks are being laid from one end only then the coping will have one less bed joint than the number of bricks being laid. To safeguard the end bricks from being accidently dislodged it is good practice to build in metal cramps, as shown in Figure 2.45.

Brick-on-edge and tile creasing is shown in Figure 2.46. This method consists of two courses of creasing tiles and a brick-on-edge laid on the top. The bottom course of the creasing tiles should be laid with the line at the lower edge of the tile. This is called the *eye line.* Then the upper course should be laid with the line at the upper edge of the tiles. With this type of work each brick is usually bedded or 'buttered' before laying. This is known as a *buttered* joint.

Sometimes roofing tiles are used on the lower course instead of creasing tiles and the nibs left showing, as illustrated in Figure 2.47. This gives an added decorative feature.

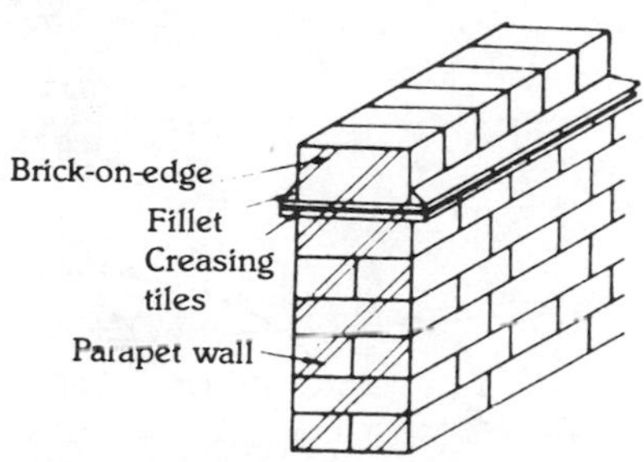

Figure 2.46 Brick-on-edge and tile creasing

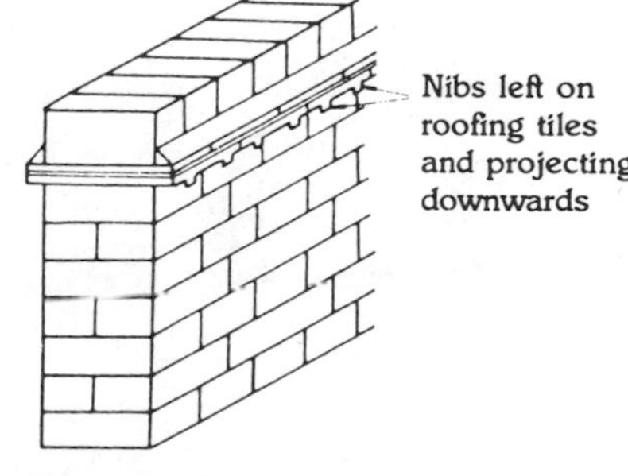

Figure 2.47 Brick-on-edge and tile creasing using roofing tiles

Tolerances

The important thing to remember when laying brick copings is that they must be kept perfectly straight along the top and along the face within a tolerance of ± 4 mm.

They should have regular joint thickness with a variance not exceeding ± 3 mm.

Questions for you

16. Explain why a coping is placed on top of a wall.

17. Draw sections showing:
(a) saddle-back coping
(b) feather-edge coping

18. A metal cramp is used for:
(a) cramping the bricks together when carrying them from the central stack to the place of working
(b) preventing the brick-on-edge coping from being accidently dislodged at a stopped end
(c) fixing a datum peg to a wall

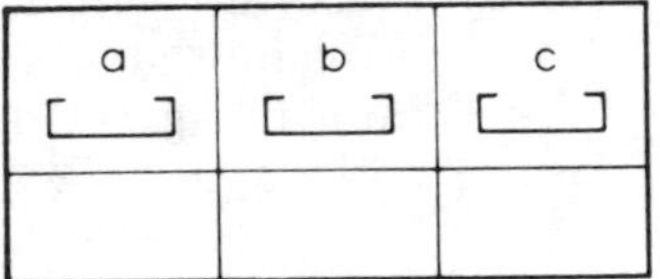

Parapet walls

Parapet walls are subjected to severe weather conditions; it is therefore recommended that bricks having a low sulphate content should be used for this work. The mortar should be a mix of sulphate resisting cement, lime and sand to a ratio of 1 : 1 : 6. This is because these walls are subjected to alternate periods of wetting and drying, so they are subject to the formation of crystals, which in turn are deposited on the face of the bricks due to the evaporation of the water. This is called *efflorescence* and appears as a white powder. If Portland cement is used in the mortar it is likely to be attacked by these crystals, causing the mortar to break down and the wall to be seriously affected. This is commonly called *sulphate attack.*

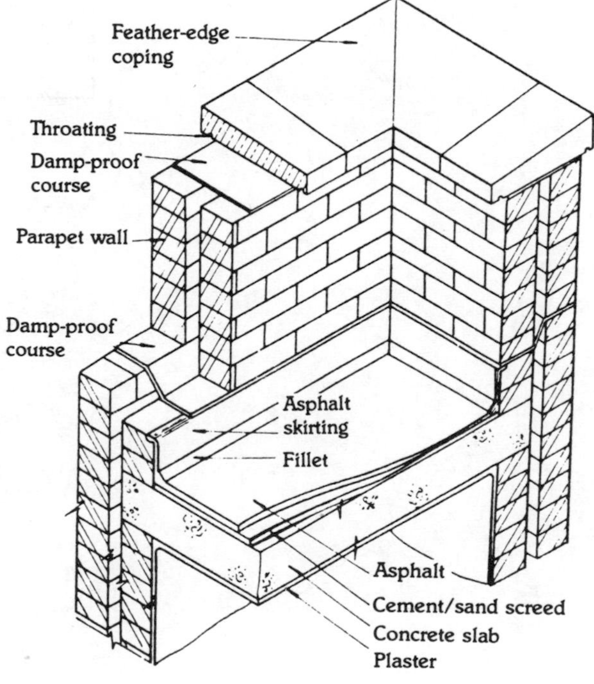

Figure 2.48 An internal angle of a parapet wall and the method of keeping dampness out of a building

A d.p.c. should be placed 150 mm above the roof surface to prevent water from penetrating downwards within the brickwork into the rooms situated immediately below the roof (Figure 2.48). It is considered good practice to insert a further d.p.c. immediately below the coping stones to prevent the parapet wall itself becoming saturated. Because these walls are subjected to wetting and drying out they expand and shrink. This *drying shrinkage* can cause cracking. In order to allow for this, *movement joints* are built into the wall in order to control the position of the cracking. The joints are usually about 40 mm wide and filled with a mastic. Sometimes they are recessed so that one section of the wall slides behind the other.

Questions for you

19. State why it is desirable to use bricks which have a low sulphate content in parapet walls.

20. Efflorescence is:
(a) an admixture put in mortar to make it more workable
(b) a white powder seen on the face of a wall
(c) a substance for cleaning off coping stones after they are laid

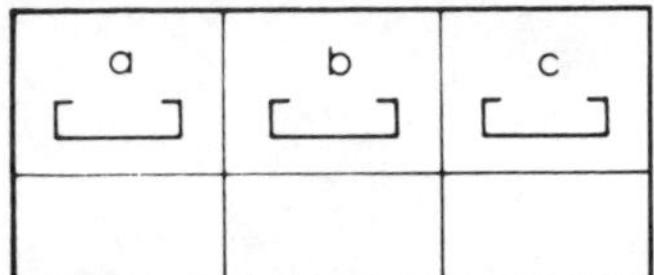

Reinforced brickwork

Brickwork is very weak in tension but extremely strong under compression. Therefore, when any pulling force is applied to walling such as at a gate post, brick lintel or walling which has a sideways thrust, such as from a pitched roof on to the wall, it is usual to give added strength to the wall by using some form of reinforcement. The position of this reinforcement must conform to the drawing and specification.

Figure 2.49 shows an expanded metal reinforcement. This type of reinforcement is supplied in rolls of varying widths for different thicknesses of walls. Figure 2.50 shows alternative types of reinforcement, namely hoop iron and mild steel rods.

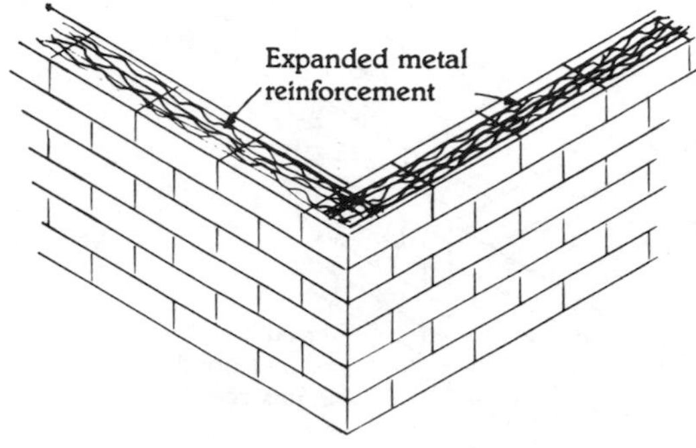

Figure 2.49 Lapping of reinforcement at a quoin

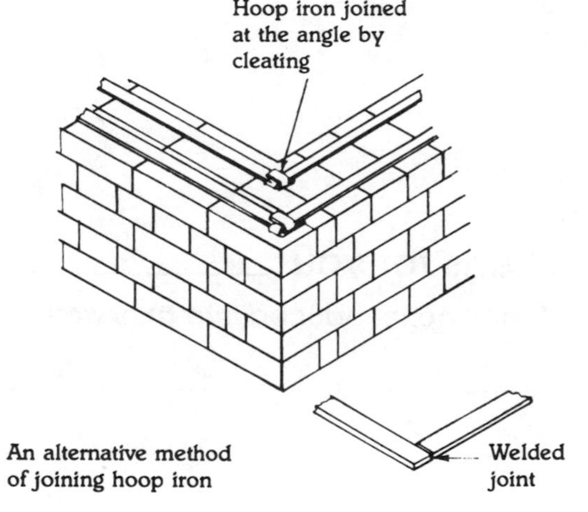

One 6 mm or 9 mm mild steel rod

Plan showing alternative method of placing reinforcement

Figure 2.50 Reinforced brickwork

In order to avoid possible detachment of the reinforcement from the mortar which may allow the reinforcement to slide through the joints, or *creep*, these precautions should be observed.

- The wire or rods should be securely bedded in the mortar.
- The reinforcement should be well-lapped at joins, corners and junctions with a minimum lap of 225 mm.
- When hoop iron is used, the ends should be cleated or even spot-welded, as shown in Figure 2.50.

Thin reinforcing rods may also be used for the strengthening of brickwork such as in a quetta bond (Figure 2.51) or at a gatepost (Figures 2.52, 2.53).

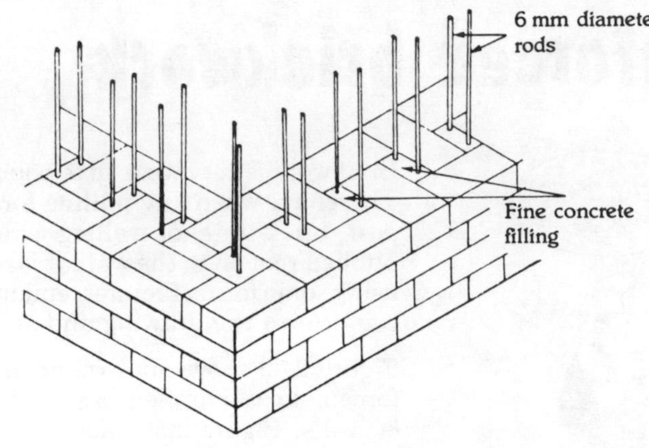

Figure 2.51 Quetta bond

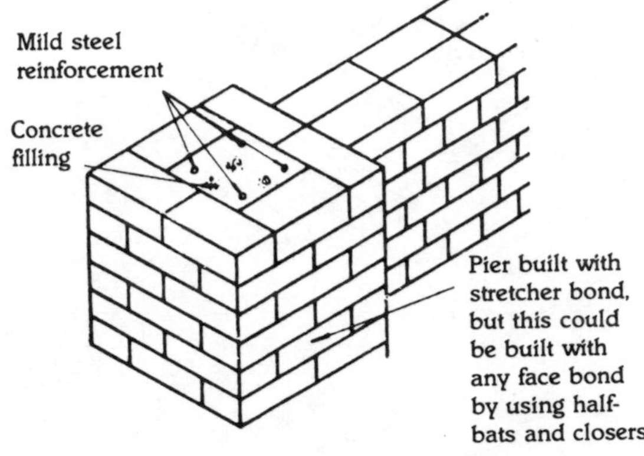

Figure 2.52 An attached pier suitable for supporting a heavy gate

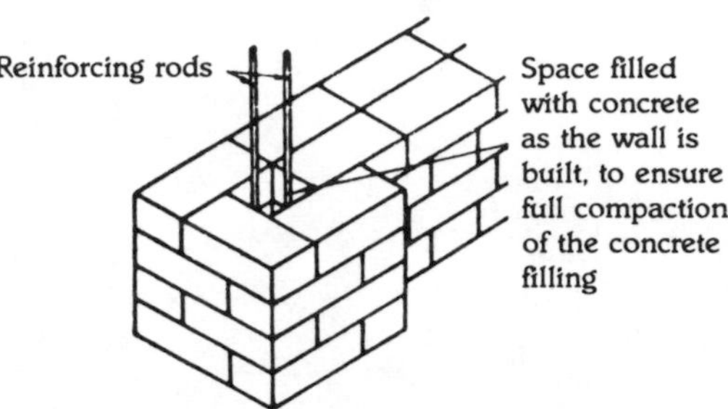

Figure 2.53 An alternative method of reinforcing a gate pier

Questions for you

21. State why reinforcement may be introduced into brickwork.

22. Describe **TWO** types of reinforcement.

Bridging openings

A simple method of bridging an opening is to use reinforced concrete lintels. These are described later in Chapter 3. If the wall is thick and the opening very wide, then the weight of a precast reinforced lintel becomes too heavy to manhandle, and some mechanical means must be used to hoist it into position. Alternatively, the lintel may be cast *in situ,* and a suitable type of formwork is shown in Figure 2.54.

Another common method of bridging openings is to use steel lintels, which are lighter than concrete and are so shaped that the face brickwork may be carried over the opening, thus avoiding having an unsightly concrete lintel showing on the facework (Figure 2.55).

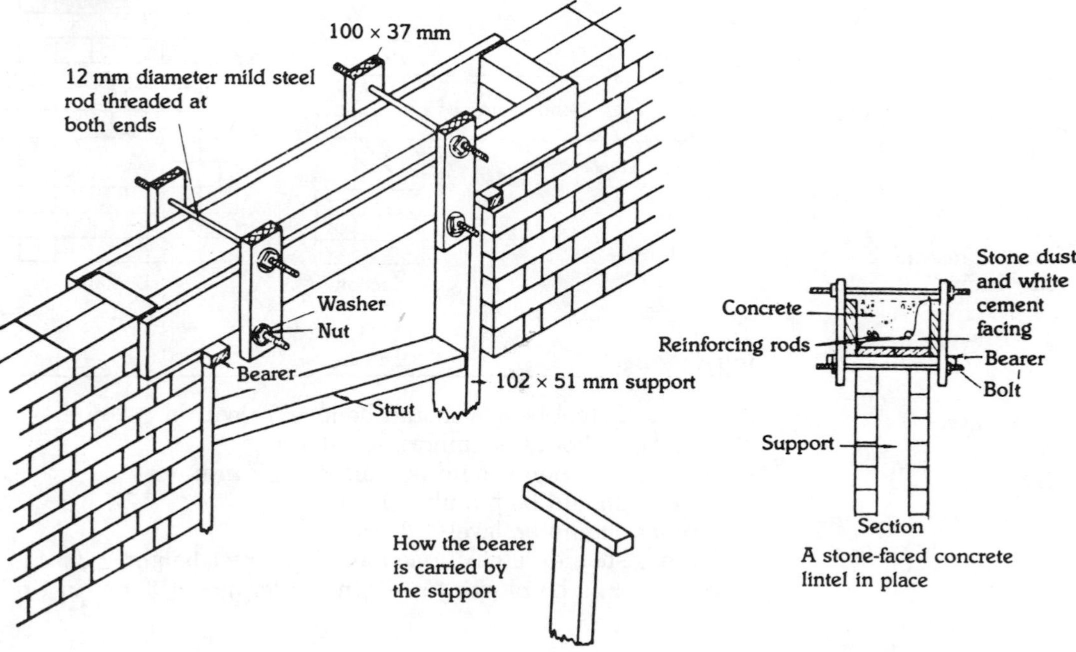

Figure 2.54 Formwork suitable for *in situ* lintels

Figure 2.55 Steel lintel

Position of lintel

If the door or window frames are fixed in the brickwork as the walling is being built then there is no difficulty in determining the correct height at which the lintel is to be laid, as it will be placed at the top of the frame. If, however, the frame is to be fixed after the walling is completed, then it is essential that the correct height of the lintel is carefully determined before being laid in position. Positioning errors are very difficult to correct at a later stage. See Chapter 3 for fixing door and window frames.

Padstones

When fixing heavy beams into walling it is usual to distribute the loading over a greater area than the immediate brickwork. This is done by placing the beam on a padstone, as shown in Figure 2.56.

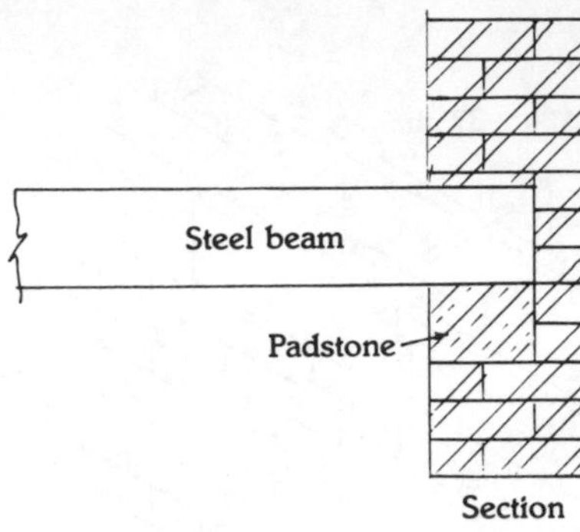

Figure 2.56 Padstone supporting beam

Tolerances

Lintels and steel beams should be level to within ± 2 mm.
The bearing should be uniform ± 10 mm.
Horizontal position should be uniform ± 3 mm.
Padstones should be plumb ± 1 mm.
Padstones should be level ± 2 mm.
Padstones should be positioned at the correct height ± 2 mm.
Reveals should be plumb to within a tolerance ± 3 mm in 1 m.

Questions for you

23. State the difference between a precast concrete lintel and one cast *in situ*. Why would each be used?

___

___

___

24. A padstone is:
(a) a bearing stone for a steel beam
(b) a stone placed underneath a lintel
(c) a stone placed at the end of a coping

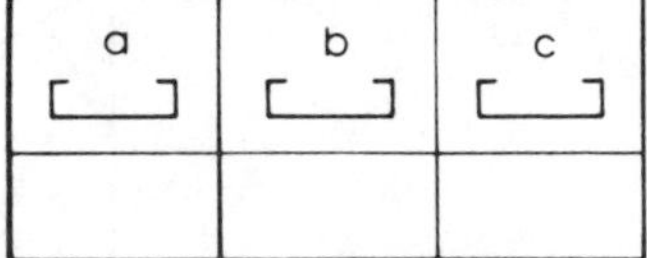

3 Half-brick walls

Stretcher bond

Figure 3.1 Stretcher bond

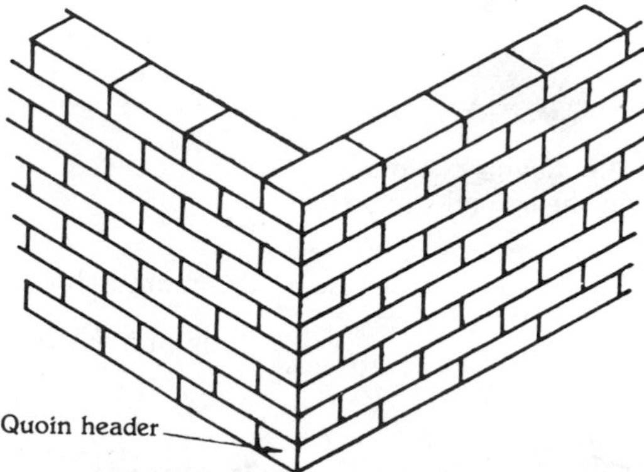

Figure 3.2 A quoin in a $\frac{1}{2}$-brick wall in stretcher bond

Stretcher bond is a straightforward bond for the building of a half-brick thick wall. All the bricks are laid as stretchers on each course and the courses are laid half bond to each other. This is effected in a plain wall by using half bats at the stopped ends on alternate courses (Figure 3.1). When building a quoin the return header forms the bond (Figure 3.2). The method of building a quoin is as follows:

1) Start the walling from a level base.
2) Mark the position of the quoin by spreading some mortar and trowelling thinly over the base (Figure 3.3).

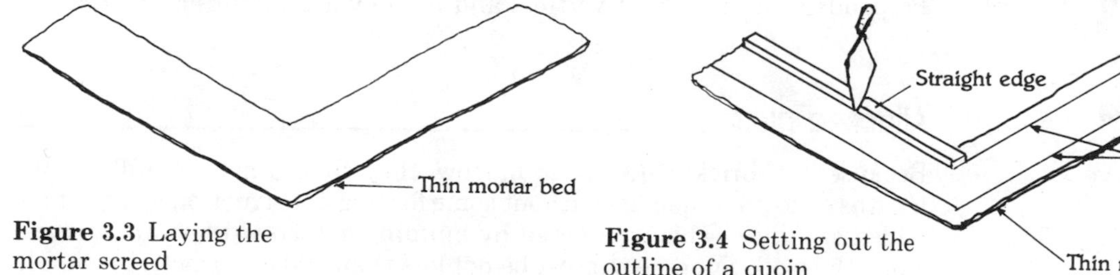

Figure 3.3 Laying the mortar screed

Figure 3.4 Setting out the outline of a quoin

3) Mark the outline of the quoin by laying a straight edge along the proposed line of the wall and, with the point of the trowel, mark the line of the wall in the mortar. Repeat for the return line (Figure 3.4).
4) Spread some mortar for the quoin header and bed the brick.
5) Check for gauge with the gauge rod (Figure 3.5).

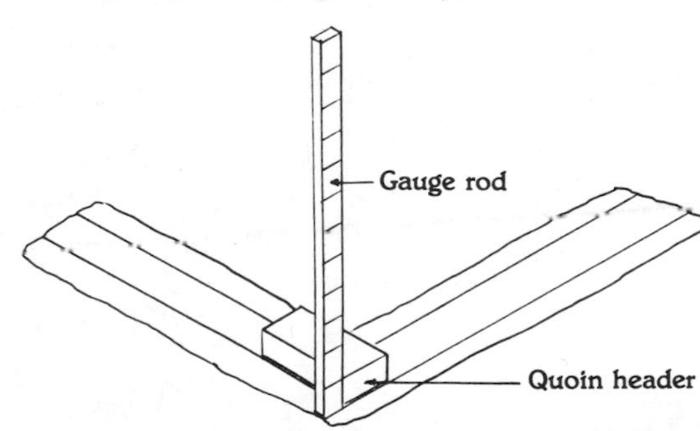

Figure 3.5 Checking for gauge with a gauge rod

6) Level the top of the brick.
7) Lay the first stretcher against the header and level.
8) Lay the quoin header in the second course and check for gauge (Figure 3.6).

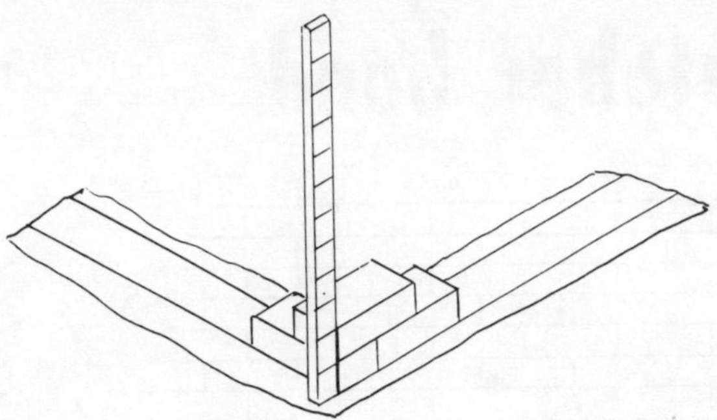

Figure 3.6 Laying the quoin header in the second course

9) Plumb the two vertical edges of the quoin with the spirit level.

This procedure is repeated for the remainder of the courses.

Tolerances

The length of the wall should be set out accurately within a tolerance of ± 3 mm in 1 m length.
The overall height of the wall should be built to gauge and with regular joint thicknesses within a tolerance of ± 5 mm in 3 m height.
The wall should be built level and to within a tolerance of ± 3 mm in a 2 m length.
The wall should be kept plumb to within ± 3 mm in 1 m height.
The face of the wall should be kept straight and should not deviate more than 5 mm.
The thickness of the perpends should be 10 mm ± 3 mm.
Perpends should be kept vertical and not deviate more than 5 mm.

Attached piers

Because half-brick walls are so narrow, they should not be built in long lengths or to great heights without some form of construction to give them added stability. This is effected by building *attached piers* at intervals along the wall. Such piers must be not less than 100 mm thick and should be well and truly bonded into the main walling, otherwise maximum stability cannot be obtained. Figure 3.7 shows the bonding of various sizes of attached piers into half-brick walls. Further examples of attached piers are illustrated in Chapter 4.

Figure 3.7 Methods of bonding attached piers into $\frac{1}{2}$-brick walls

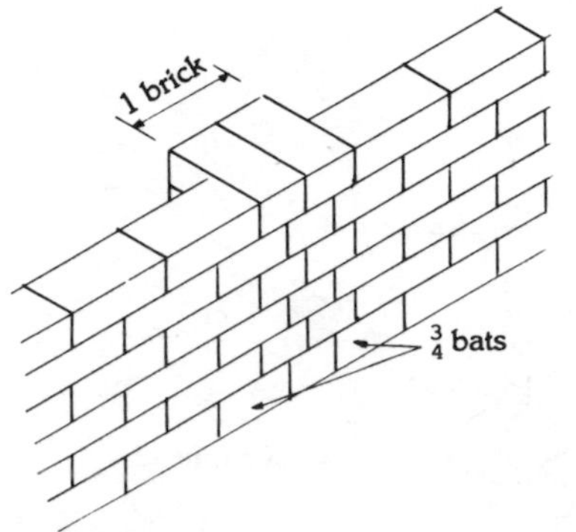

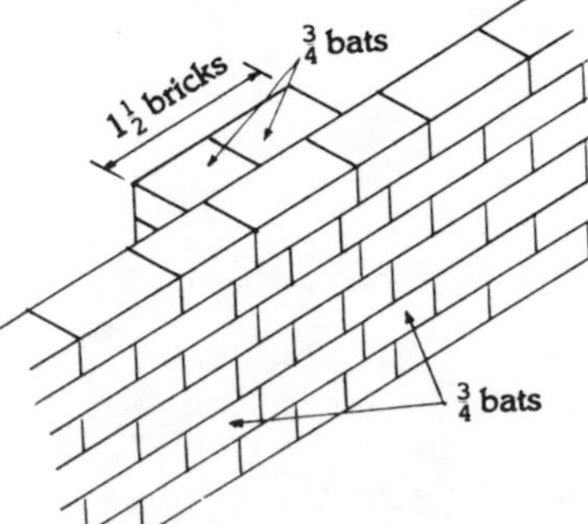

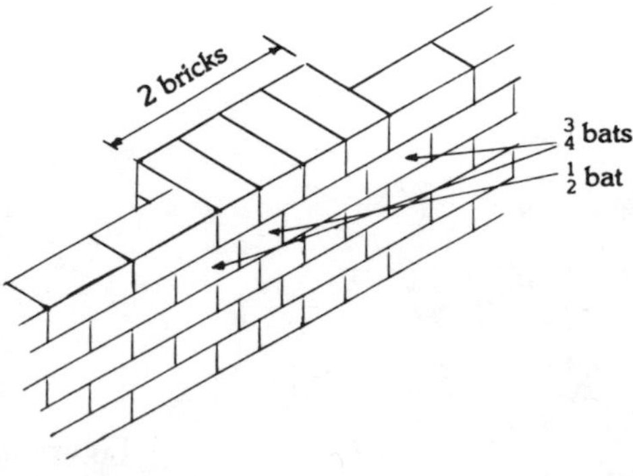

The tops of the piers may be finished off by *tumbling-in*. This not only gives a decorative finish but provides a *weathering* or slope to protect the top of the pier against the effects of the weather. Figure 3.8 shows examples of tumbling-in.

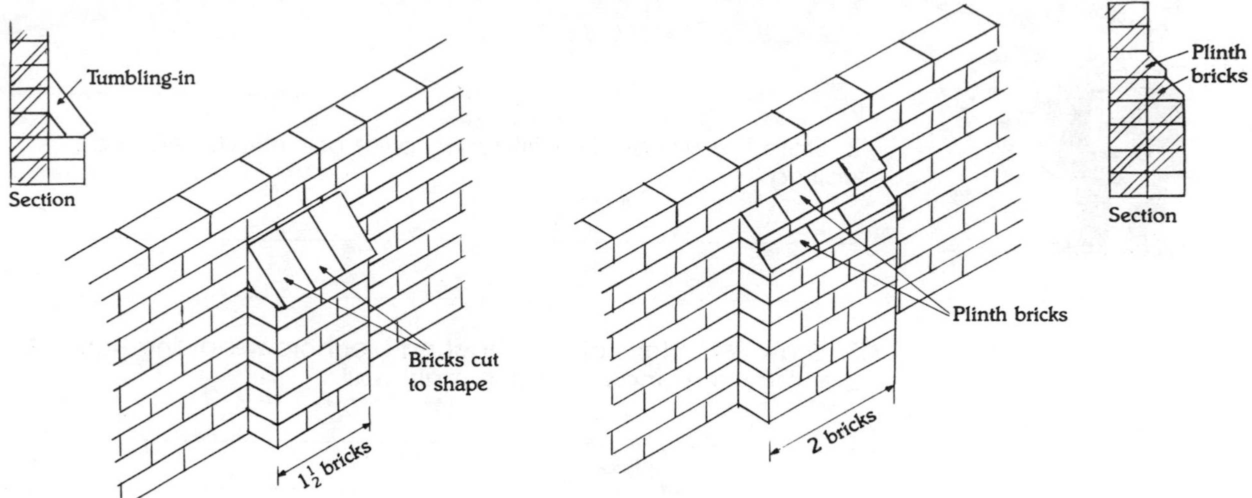

Figure 3.8 Tumbling-in attached piers

Junction walls

In order to achieve the maximum stability, a junction wall must be well bonded into the main wall. Difficulty may often be encountered in trying to avoid straight joints occurring in the facework. Therefore it is quite usual to introduce three-quarter bats as shown in Figure 3.9.

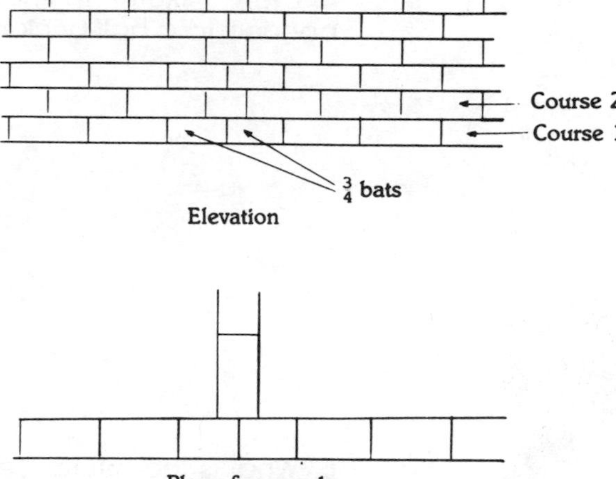

Plan of course 1

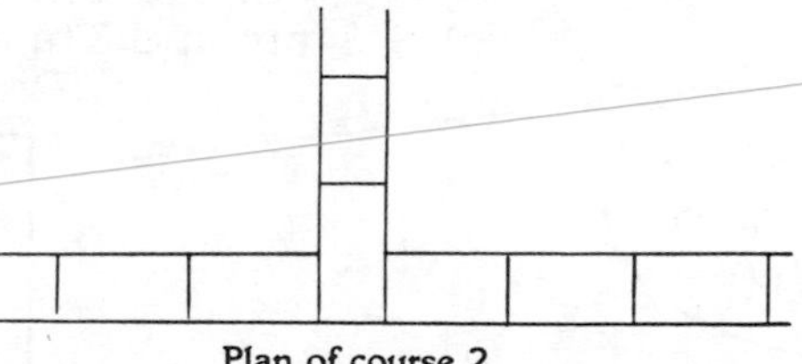

Figure 3.9 Bonding of a $\frac{1}{2}$-brick junction wall into a $\frac{1}{2}$-brick main wall

Questions for you

1. Describe how to set out a quoin before any bricks are laid.

2. State the reason that attached piers are introduced into walling.

3. Draw **TWO** plans of the attached pier below showing how the pier may be bonded into the main wall.

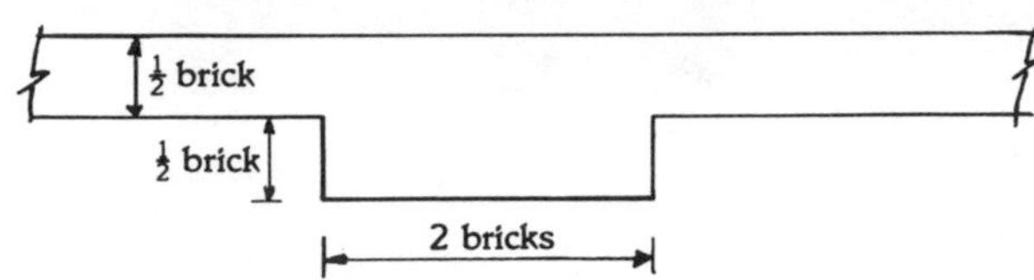

4. Draw a sketch to show how a half-brick junction wall may be bonded to a half-brick main wall.

5. What is the tolerance allowed for the levelling of a wall?
(a) ±2 mm in a 3 m length
(b) ±3 mm in a 2 m length
(c) ±3 mm in a 3 m length

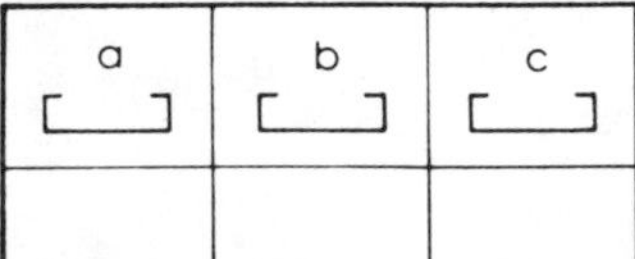

Openings in half-brick walling

The forming of openings in half-brick walling is quite straightforward. The *jambs* or *reveals* must be kept plumb and the bonding to the walling each side worked out before building commences. This is to ensure that the bonding works out to even brick sizes. If it does not, then a *broken bond* must be introduced at the centre of the pier. If the opening is for a window then the walling immediately below the opening may also require a broken bond. Figure 3.10 shows an example of setting out the bond for an opening, and piers each side of an opening where they do not conform to brick sizes. Note how the bond is set out at the base of the wall.

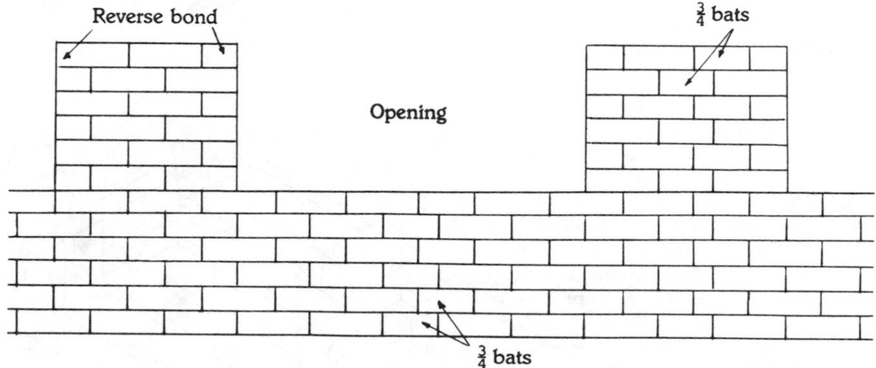

Figure 3.10 Setting out the bond for a window opening and piers

A *pinch bar or rod* is a very useful tool which is cut to the exact width of an opening so that its width can be readily checked at the stage of the construction by running the pinch rod up and down. If it fouls the jambs then the opening will be too tight for the frame to be fitted. There should be a pinch rod for each width of opening on a site. This is really a managerial tool, to enable the foreman to make a quick check on the openings as the work is proceeding.

Reinforced concrete lintels

The simplest way to bridge an opening is by using a reinforced concrete lintel. These are extremely efficient for bridging openings but they must be placed so that the steel reinforcement is positioned at the *bottom* of the lintel to resist tensile stresses. The concrete is strong enough to resist the compressive stresses as shown in Figure 3.11. It is common practice to mark these lintels 'top' with a sharp tool in the wet concrete when they are cast.

Figure 3.11 Bridging an opening

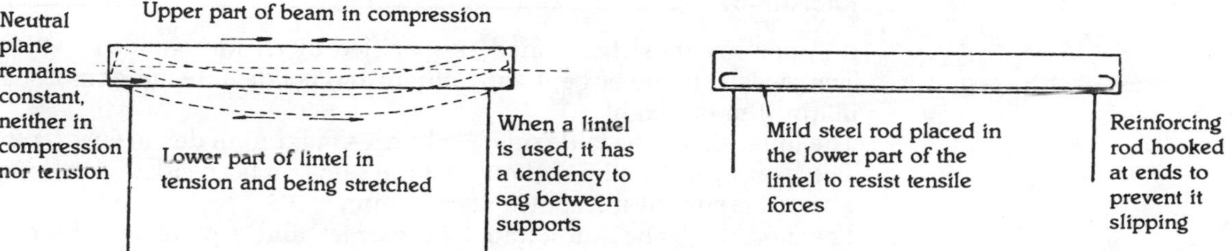

A simple method of casting a concrete lintel for a half-brick wall is shown in Figure 3.12. If a large number of lintels are required for a job, then these may be cast in batches; Figure 3.13 shows a simple system for setting up the formwork in which they can be cast.

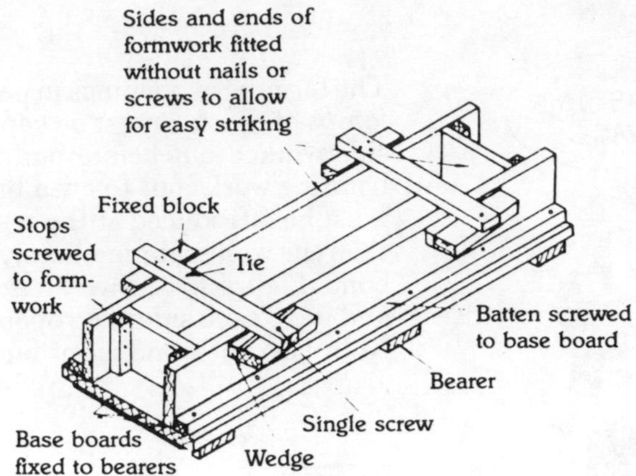

Figure 3.12 Formwork suitable or precast lintels

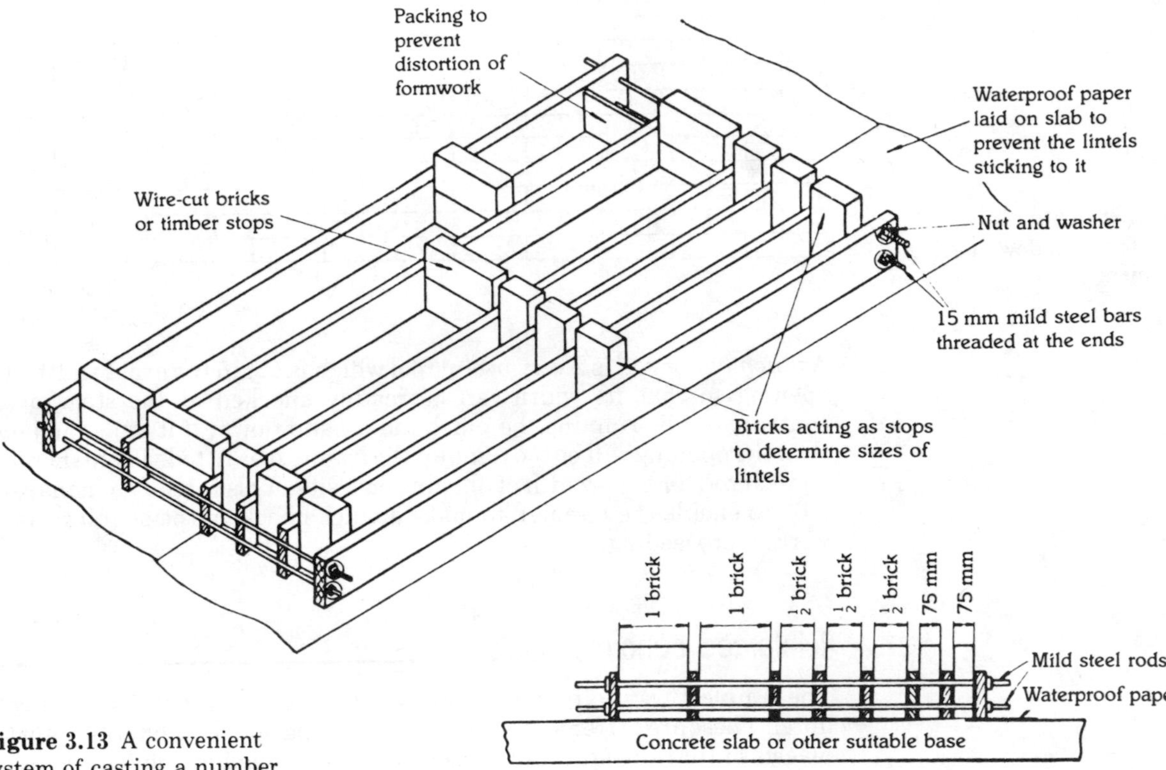

End view showing how lintels of various sizes may be cast with this system

Figure 3.13 A convenient system of casting a number of lintels in one operation. This system may also be used for casting lintels of different lengths and widths

Tolerances

All openings must be formed as specified by the designer.
The reveals should be kept truly plumb and not deviate more than ± 3 mm in any 1 m of height.
The lintel should be laid truly level with a maximum deviation of ± 2 mm.
The bearing of the lintel should be the same on both sides of the opening with a maximum difference of ± 10 mm.
The height of the lintel must be correct and not deviate more than ± 3 mm.

Fixing frames

Frames may be fixed either
- as the wall is being built, or
- after the wall has been completed.

Fixing during building. Fixing the frame as the walling is being built is more convenient for the bricklayer, since the frame acts as a profile and reduces the amount of plumbing that would otherwise be necessary.

The frame should be held in place with the aid of *two* boards, one at each side of the frame, in order to ensure that the frame remains parallel to the face of the wall from bottom to top and also that it is kept plumb during building operations. Each board may be secured at its base by means of bricks or other heavy objects, and the frame may be held at its head by a block nailed on the board, or by nails projecting from the board and hitched over the head of the frame. It is also very important to ensure that the frame is not squeezed in at the middle, particularly with frames of small cross-section. To prevent this happening, it is a good practice to fix a length of batten known as a *stretcher* across the centre of the frame (Figure 3.14).

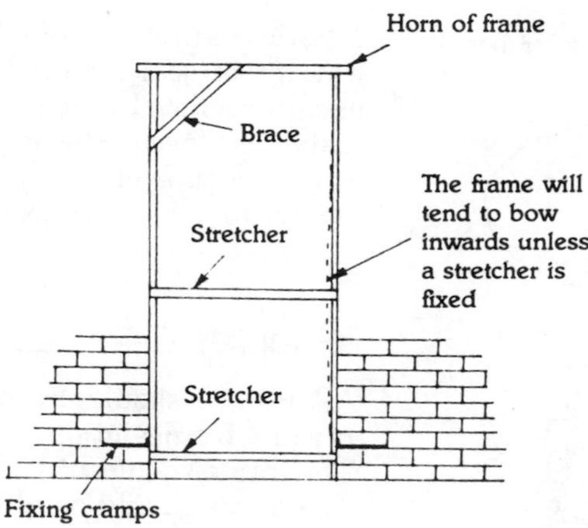

Figure 3.14 An elevation showing a method of preventing distortion in a frame during building-in operations

Great care must be taken to ensure that the frame is kept truly plumb while it is being built into the wall. It is very costly and time-wasting to correct a frame which has been built into position without being properly plumbed.

If the frame is to be fixed as the work is being built, then the frame may be secured with door cramps, as shown in Figure 3.15. The ends of the cramps may be fish-tailed or bent over into the joint.

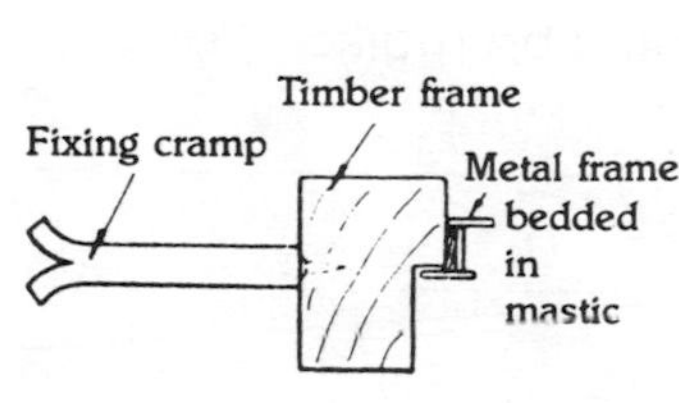

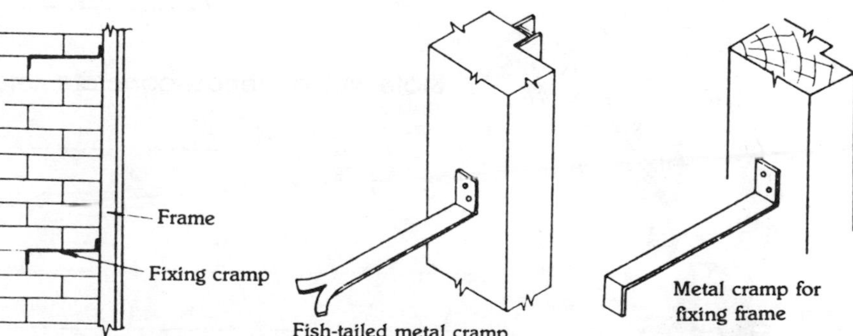

Figure 3.15 Fixing timber frames

Fixing after building. If the frames are to be secured after the wall is built, then provision must be made for their fixing. This may be done by building a brick in sand at intervals up the reveal. When the frame is to be put into position the sand course is removed and the frame can then be secured with cramps and the brickwork built into place. Another method is to build fixing bricks or wooden pads at every 600 mm in the reveal. These should be laid so that their grain runs across the wall (Figure 3.16).

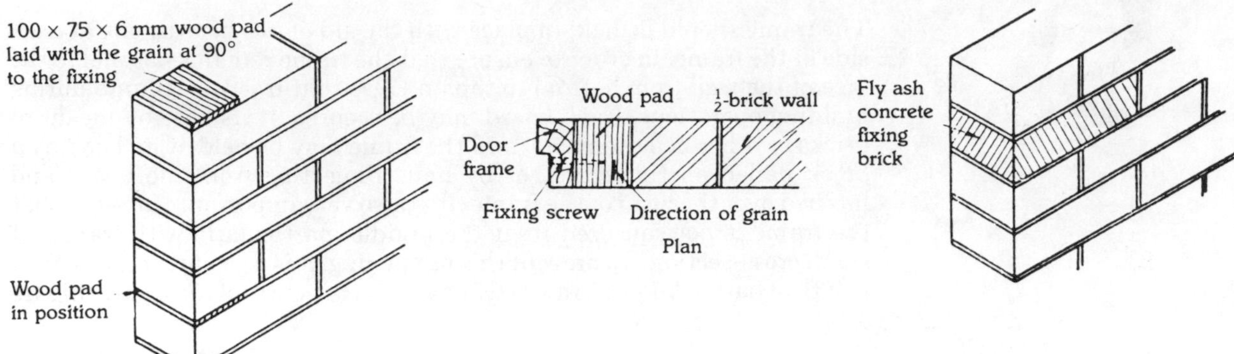

Figure 3.16 Fixing timber door frames

Mastic sealant is applied between the frame and the jamb to provide the waterproof seal required on the outside of a building. The sealant is usually applied by means of a 'gun' which is a tool into which a tube of the sealant is placed. The handle is applied so that the sealant is squeezed out as from a tube of toothpaste. There is a wide variety of sealants on the market to suit all kinds of work and conditions.

Tolerances

All frames should be positioned as indicated on the drawings with permissible deviation to suit the bond or thickness of perpends.
The frame should be the correct height – 2 mm.
The frame should be plumb in both directions ± 2 mm in full height.

Questions for you

TRY AND ANSWER THESE

6. A broken bond should be:
(a) placed at the side of an opening or pier
(b) placed in the middle of an opening or pier
(c) lost by making the perpends in a wall thicker or thinner

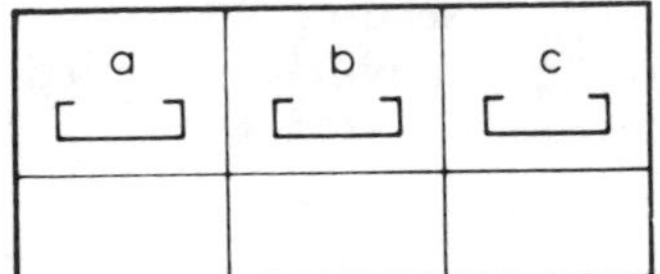

a	b	c

7. State why a precast concrete lintel should be marked 'top'.

Cutting to a rake

Stretcher bond is quite popular for the building of garden walls and special features are often introduced into such work for decoration. One interesting method is to form a *ramp*. This is simple enough to build but special care must be taken with the cutting of the bricks. The easiest way of cutting is with a brick-cutting saw and there are many efficient types of these machines on the market. If such a saw is not readily available and the bricks have to be cut by hand then great care must be taken with the cutting if excessive waste is to be avoided. There are two methods of cutting bricks by hand.

The first method is shown in Figure 3.17 and may be carried out as follows:

1) The brick is first marked where it is to be cut. This may be easily done with the aid of an adjustable bevel, the blade of which may be used for marking the angle of cut for all the bricks.
2) The first cut with a hammer and bolster is at right angles to the bed of the brick.

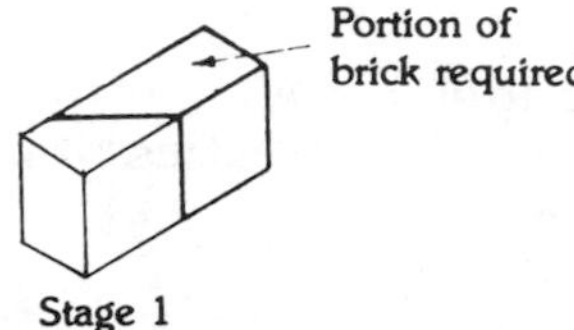

Stage 1

The brick is marked out for a cut

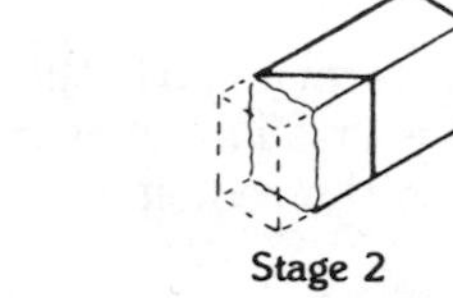

Stage 2

The brick is cut with a hammer and bolster at right angles to its face

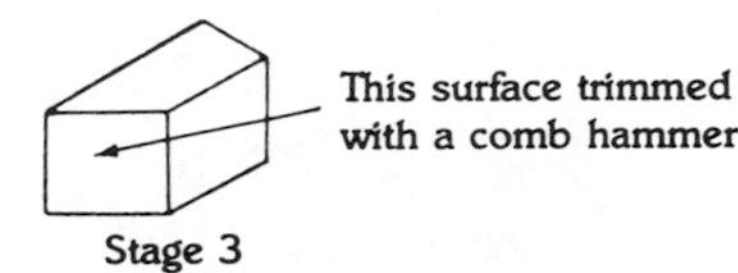

Stage 3

The brick is cut along the splayed line and the face of the cut trimmed to an even surface

Figure 3.17 Cutting bricks with a bolster and hammer

3) The brick is then cut along the splayed line and the cut surface of the brick is then trimmed off with a comb hammer.

The second method is to mark the splay from the end of the brick and when this has been trimmed, cut the brick to its required length (Figure 3.18).

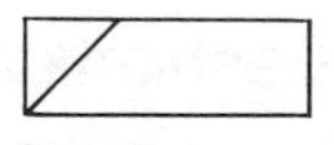

Stage 1
The brick is marked

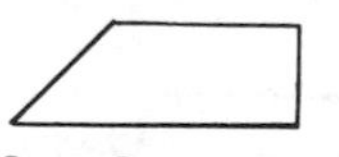

Stage 2
The splayed end is cut

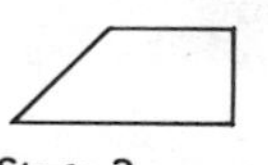

Stage 3
The brick is cut to the required length

Figure 3.18 Alternative method of cutting bricks

To build the rake, a length of batten is fixed to the wall and a line is set to the required angle of the rake (Figure 3.19). The bricks can then be bedded to the line as required.

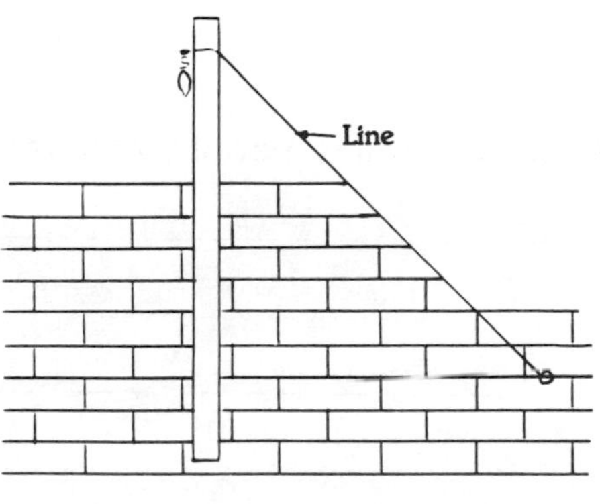

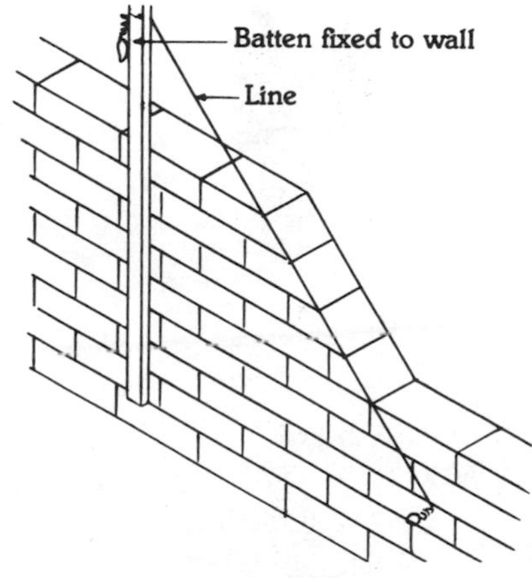

Figure 3.19 Cutting a ramp

Lining up a gable. Cutting to a rake is also necessary for the end wall of a building, or for a gable end, which is to be cut to the same slope as the roof. The latter is commonly called *lining up a gable.* This is carried out by erecting two temporary rafters with a short length of ridge board and bracing, as shown in Figure 3.20. A line is then stretched from the *springing,* the starting point of the gable, to the ridge board. The bricks may then be marked, cut and laid to the line.

Figure 3.20 A method of lining-up a gable

Beamfilling is the term given to the building up of the walling between the rafters and/or the joists. This construction assists in preventing birds from gaining access into the roof space.

Tolerances

When cutting to a rake all raking cuts should be in line and deviate not more than ± 3 mm in a 1 m length.
The face plan of the raking cuts should match the existing wall ± 2 mm in 1 m length.
The raking cuts should be built in the same gauge as the wall ± 1 mm.

Questions for you

8. Describe a method of building a brick ramp.

____

____

____

____

9. Describe what is meant by the term 'lining up a gable'.

____

____

____

____

4 Isolated and attached piers

Isolated piers

Isolated piers should be set out so that they are regular in shape. A wooden square may be used for setting out the pier internally or a steel square may be used to check the external angles, as shown in Figure 4.1. Generally, isolated piers should be built with hard burnt bricks with a mortar of cement/lime/sand mix in the proportions 1 : 1 : 5 or 1 : 1 : 6.

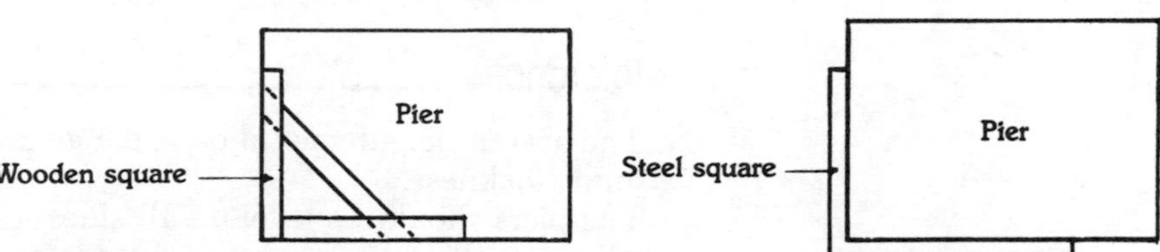

Figure 4.1 Setting out a pier using a wooden or steel square

If the piers are to carry heavy loads, then they may be built with dense engineering bricks which should be bedded in a strong mortar of Portland cement and sand in the ratio 1 : 4. A pier built purely for decorative purposes may be left hollow, which will save bricks. If the interior is filled with bricks then the pier has a *brick core.* Similarly, if it is filled with concrete it has a *concrete core.*

The loading to which the pier is to be subjected will determine the type of structure. If the loading is very heavy and likely to introduce bending stresses, then reinforcing rods should be introduced into the concrete core to resist the tensile stresses. When building isolated piers great care should be taken to ensure that the height of the pier is not too great for the cross-sectional area, otherwise the pier will become unstable. These piers should be built to the correct size to suit the bond, as it is bad practice to have a broken bond in such a construction.

A simple one-brick square pier is shown in Figure 4.2. Two methods of building one-and-a-half-brick square pier are shown in Figure 4.3. The first method allows easy placing of the reinforcement and filling in with a fine concrete. The second shows the bonding of a pier using English bond. Figure 4.4 shows the bonding of a two-brick square pier in English bond and Figure 4.5 shows the same sized pier in Flemish bond. Note the use of three-quarter bats in the Flemish bond and closers in the English bond.

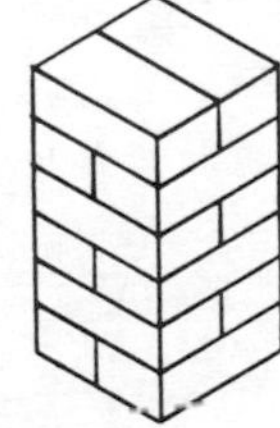

Figure 4.2 A 1-brick isolated pier

Figure 4.3 Two methods of building a $1\frac{1}{2}$-brick isolated pier in English bond

Figure 4.4 A 2-brick isolated pier built in English bond

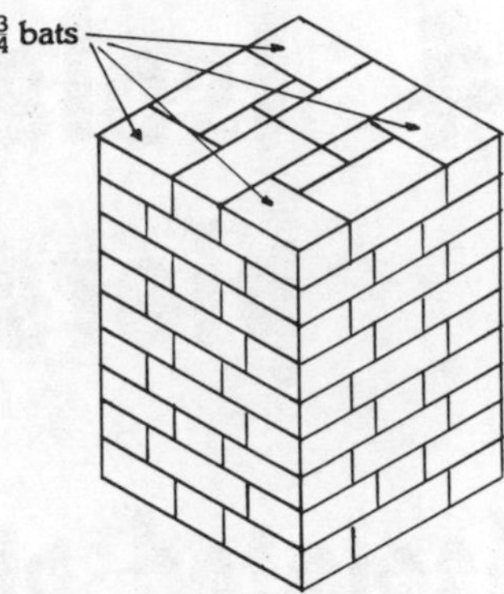

Figure 4.5 A 2-brick isolated pier built in Flemish bond

To estimate the number of bricks in a pier, calculate the number of bricks in one course and multiply by the number of courses.

Tolerances

The overall height should be to gauge ± 5 mm in 3 m height with regular joint thickness.
The piers should be level on all sides ± 2 mm.
All points should be plumb within a tolerance of ± 3 mm in any 1 m height.
No face shall deviate more than 3 mm on any side.

Questions for you

1. Sketch a one-and-a-half brick square pier showing how it may be strengthened if it is intended to be used as a gate pillar.

2. To bond a two-brick square pier in English bond requires:
(a) three-quarter bats
(b) closers
(c) half bats

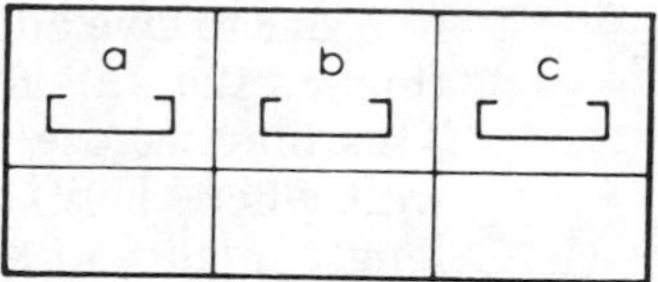

3. An isolated pier is to carry a heavy load. The recommended materials to be used are:
(a) soft bricks in a cement/lime/sand mix 1 : 1 : 8
(b) facing bricks in a cement/lime/sand mix 1 : 1 : 9
(c) dense or engineering bricks in a cement/sand mix 1 : 4

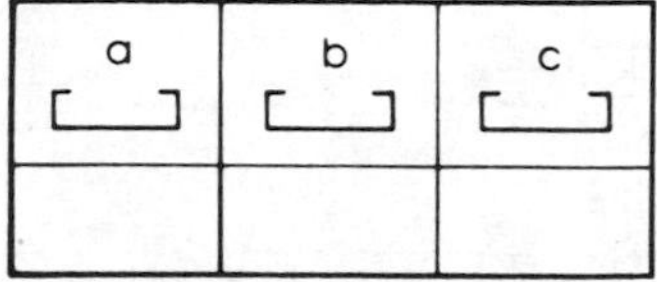

4. Draw **TWO** plans of a two-brick square isolated pier showing the bonding of alternate courses in Flemish bond.

Attached piers

In order to give added lateral strength to a wall it is common practice to thicken the wall at intervals along its length, as described in Chapter 3. This practice uses *attached piers.* A typical example of this is a garage wall, where there is little weight to carry but the wall may be weak along its length. Figure 4.6 shows how such a wall may be built and how the piers are bonded into the main wall in order to achieve the maximum stability. Figure 4.7 shows the bonding of a one-and-a-half-brick attached pier into a half-brick wall, and also a two-brick attached pier.

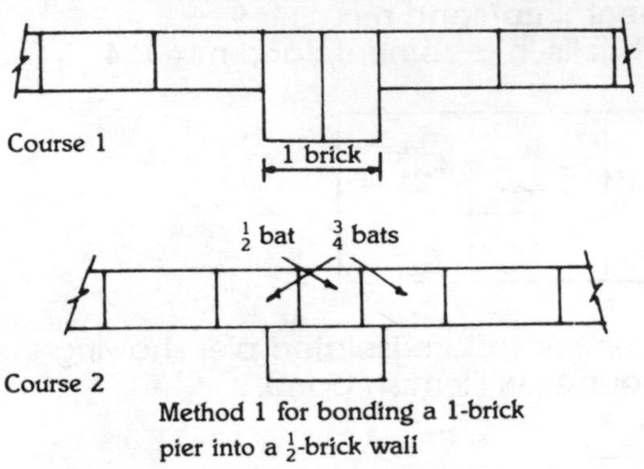

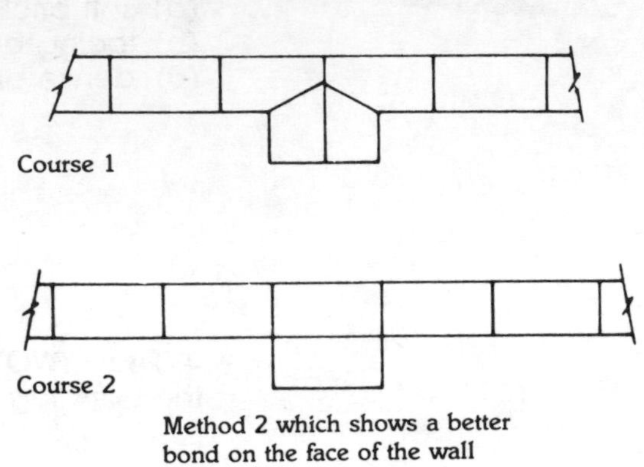

Figure 4.6 Two methods of bonding a 1-brick attached pier into a $\frac{1}{2}$-brick wall

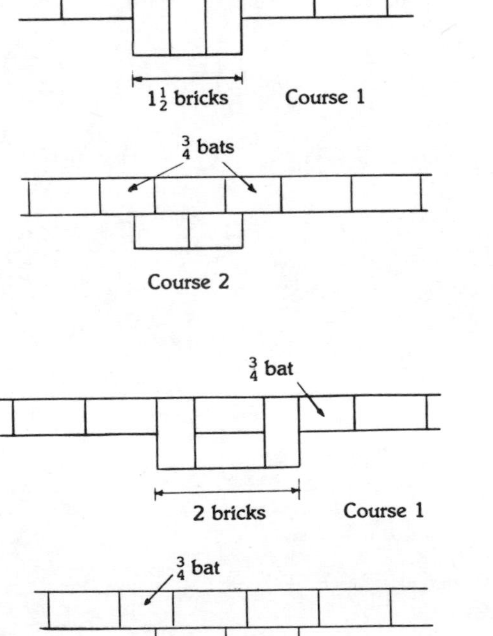

Figure 4.7 Attached piers in half-brick walling

Just as half-brick walls need side support, so do some thicker walls; Figures 4.8–4.13 show the bonding of one-and-a-half-brick and two-brick attached piers to a one-brick wall in English and Flemish bonds.

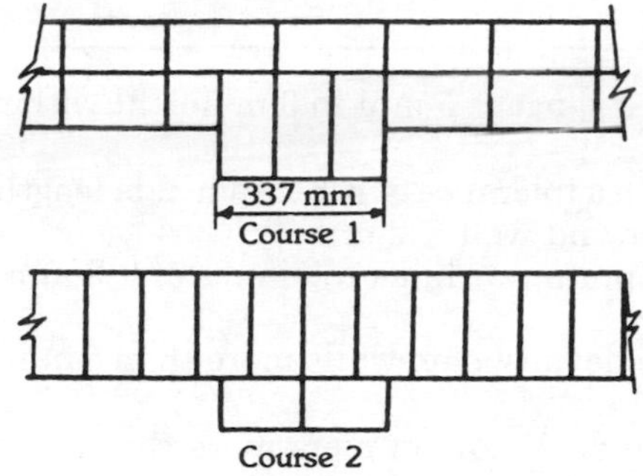

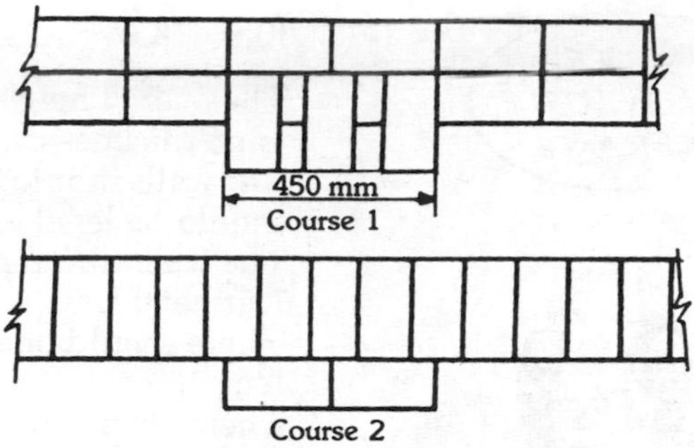

Figure 4.8 Bonding attached piers in English bond

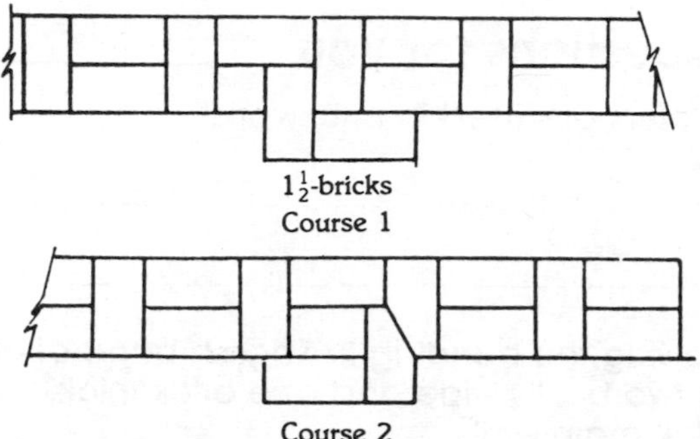

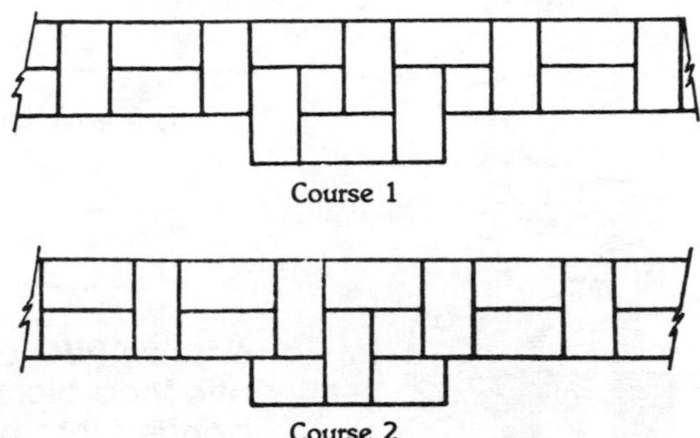

Figure 4.9 Attached piers in Flemish bond

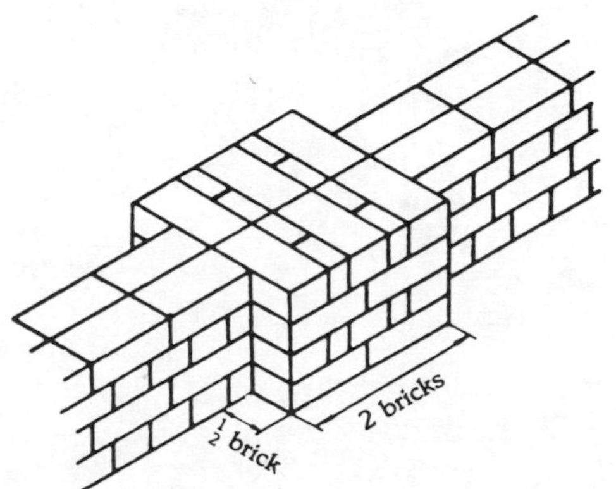

Figure 4.10 Double attached piers in English bond

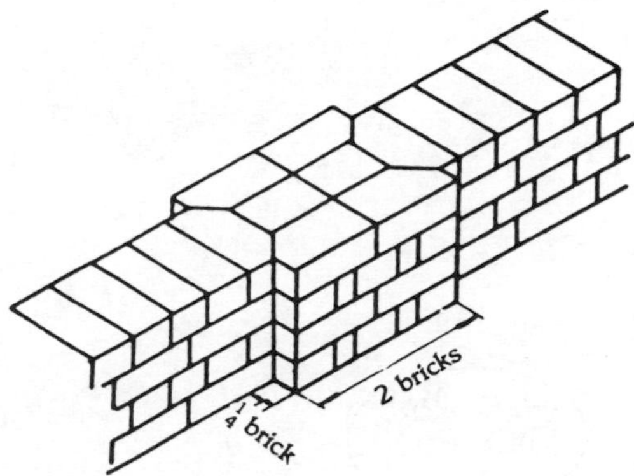

Figure 4.11 Double attached piers in English bond

Figure 4.12 Double attached piers in Flemish bond

Figure 4.13 Double attached piers in Flemish bond

Tolerances

The overall height should be to gauge ± 5 mm in 3 m height with regular joint thickness.
The walls should be level within a tolerance of ± 3 mm in 2 m length. Piers should be level across the pier and wall ± 2 mm.
The walls and piers should be plumb within a tolerance of ± 3 mm in any 1 m height.
There should be no face plane deviation on walls more than 5 mm in 3 m length.
There should be no face plane deviation on piers more than 3 mm, permitted deviations of perpends is 5 mm.

Questions for you

5. State why attached piers are used in brickwork.

____

____

6. Draw **TWO** plans showing the bonding in English bond of an attached pier which is two bricks wide and one brick thick, bonded into a one-brick main wall.

7. Tumbling-in is the term used:
(a) when the wall is raked back at a corner
(b) when cutting a rake at a gable end
(c) when finishing off the top of an attached pier

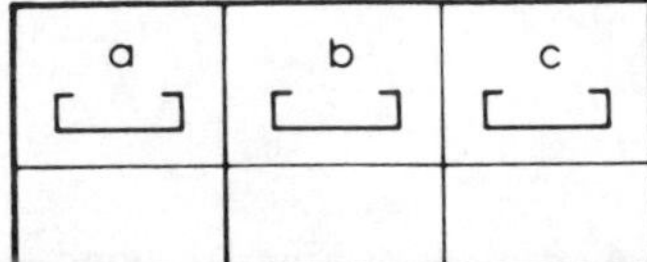

a [ ]	b [ ]	c [ ]

Jointing

In order to give the completed brickwork a pleasing appearance it is customary to give the mortar joints a *tooled* finish. When the joints are finished off as the work proceeds this is referred to as *jointing* and should be carried out as each course is laid, or possibly after every two courses if the mortar is still soft enough to allow them to be treated.

The following are some types of joint finishes which may be used:

Flush joint (Figure 4.14). This appears to be quite a simple type of joint finish but in fact is quite a difficult one to carry out if the face of the brickwork is to be kept free from mortar stains. With this type of finish it is quite usual to build a number of courses so that the mortar is comparatively hard. First ensure that there are no voids in the mortar joints and then rub the surface of the walling with a piece of hessian or similar cloth. The mortar must not be too soft or it will smear over the faces of the bricks. Conversely, it should not be too hard, otherwise it will be too difficult to finish off the joints in a tidy manner. When this type of jointing is done well it produces a very effective finish, particularly if the wall has been built with hand-made facing bricks. The cloth used for rubbing the joints should be changed frequently to prevent the face of the wall from becoming stained through using a dirty cloth.

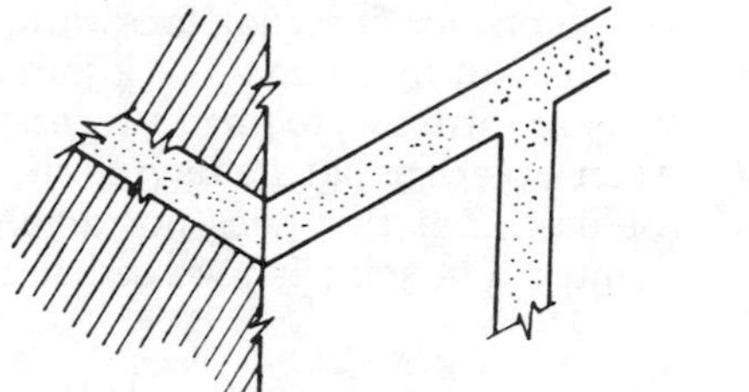

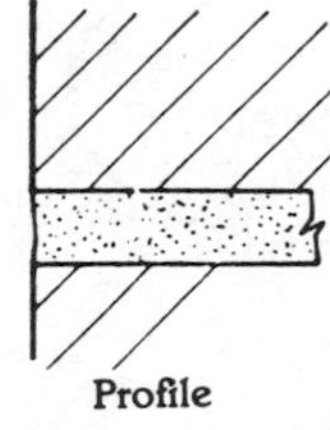

Figure 4.14 A flush joint

Struck joint (Figure 4.15). This is carried out while the mortar is still wet so each course is finished off as the work proceeds. If the mortar is not drying too quickly, then perhaps two courses may be finished at a time. Building too many courses before striking the joints may mean that the mortar sets quite hard making it very difficult to finish the joints in a neat and tidy manner. The perpends are usually treated first by rubbing the trowel on the mortar joint, pressing the mortar into one side of the joint. This is repeated on all of the perpends. The bed joints are treated in the same way but the trowel is pressed into the bottom edge of the joints. This type of finish is not really recommended for external walling as there is always a possibility that rain water may collect on the bottom edge of the joint and, if it freezes, may have a harmful effect on the bricks. However, a struck joint is ideal for use on internal facework.

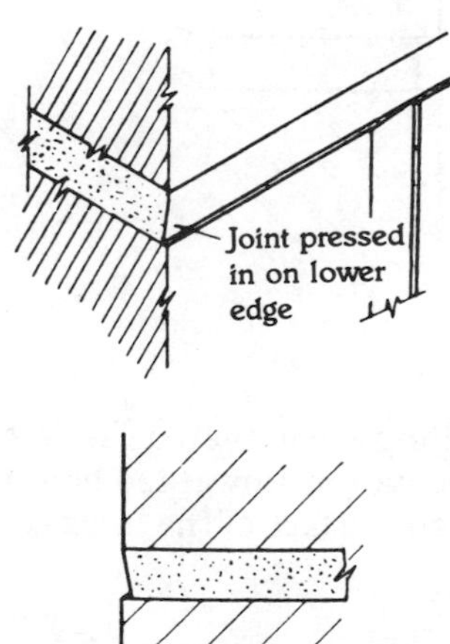

Profile

Figure 4.15 A struck joint

Weather-struck joint (Figure 4.16). This is carried out in the same manner as for struck jointing, except that in this case the trowel is pressed in at the upper edge of the joints. This gives better protection to the joints, as the mortar finish will tend to throw the rain water off the joints. This type of finish can have an even better appearance if the joints are cut off at the bottom edge by firmly holding a pointing rule or straightedge along the joint and trimming off the bottom edge with a trowel. The perpends are also cut off with a trowel in the same manner. This is called a *Struck-and-cut joint*. When this method is done well it gives a very attractive finish to the walling.

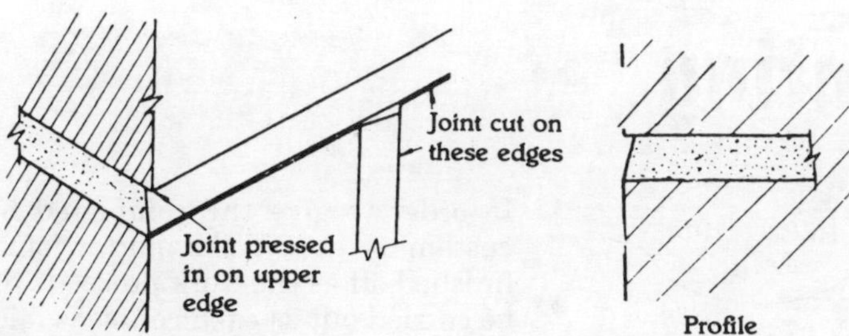

Figure 4.16 A weather-struck and cut joint

Rounded or tooled finish (Figure 4.17). This is sometimes called a *Bucket handle joint* and is a popular method of finishing off mortar joints. It is carried out by rubbing a jointing iron, which is a short length of reinforcing rod bent to the shape of a 'z', over the bed joints and the perpends while they are still soft.

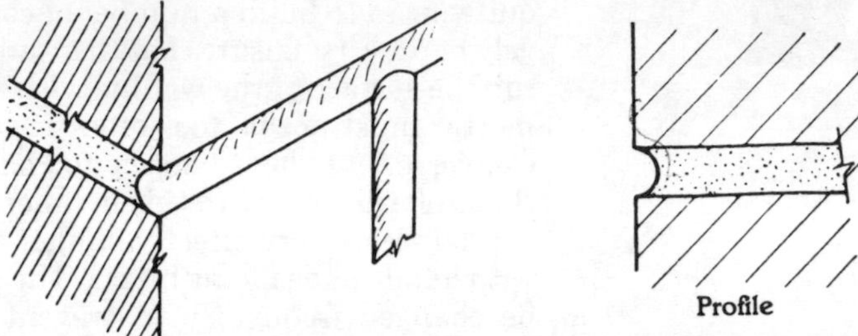

Figure 4.17 A rounded or tooled joint

A recessed joint (Figure 4.18). This is a very popular method of finishing off joints for internal facework, especially with brick fireplaces. It is carried out by using a brick jointing tool and pressing in the joints while they are still soft to form a recess. If a tuck or brick jointer is not available then a piece of batten having the same thickness as the mortar joint may be used, but this does not give the same quality of finish as the brick jointer. The joint is recessed to a depth of about 4 or 5 mm.

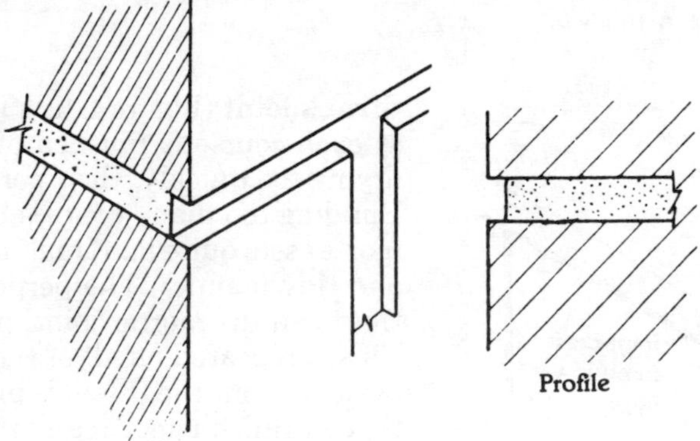

Figure 4.18 A recessed joint

Whichever type of jointing is used, once the walling is completed the face should be lightly brushed with a soft brush to remove any unwanted bits of mortar which may have been inadvertently left on the face of the bricks or the edges of the joints.

Gauging a pointing mortar

Mortars for pointing must be mixed more precisely than ordinary mortars for brickwork so as to ensure that the colour of the pointing remains the same throughout the whole of the work. The mixes of these mortars vary in composition according to requirements but as a general rule the ultimate strength of the mortar should not exceed the strength of the brick.

For hard dense bricks in exposed positions, such as parapet walls, a Portland cement and sand mix of 1 : 4 may be used, or even a sulphate-resisting cement and sand mix of the same ratio. For general facework, a cement/lime/sand mix of 1 : 1 : 6 should be quite adequate.

When coloured pointing mortars are required, then there are several factors which must be considered:

- The materials must be carefully and accurately measured. Gauge boxes may be used if measuring by volume. These are four-sided boxes with no bottom which are filled to the top and lifted off. One box may be used for each of sand, cement and lime. Alternatively, the ingredients may be measured by weighing them.
- The pigments must be applied in accordance with the manufacturer's instructions.
- The pigments are usually dust-like and should be sheltered from strong winds when being added to the mix.
- Sands vary in colour and composition, so it is essential that the same type of sand is used throughout the whole of the work.
- The ingredients should be thoroughly mixed together dry, then water added and mixed again for at least two minutes until the right consistency and colour distribution is reached.
- Since a small amount of mortar goes a long way when pointing, it is wise to mix the mortar in small quantities each time.

Questions for you

8. Jointing is the term given to:
(a) raking out the joints and filling them with a pointing mortar
(b) finishing off the joints as the work proceeds
(c) flushing in the internal joints of each course as it is laid

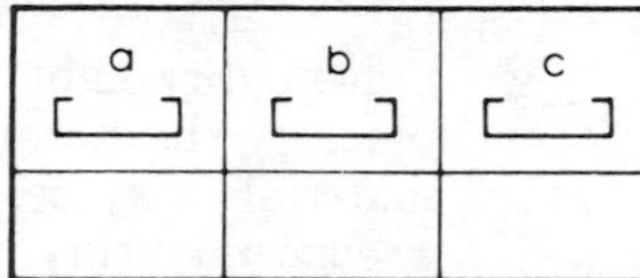

a	b	c

9. A recessed joint is one which is finished off with:
(a) a jointing iron
(b) a pointing trowel
(c) a brick jointer

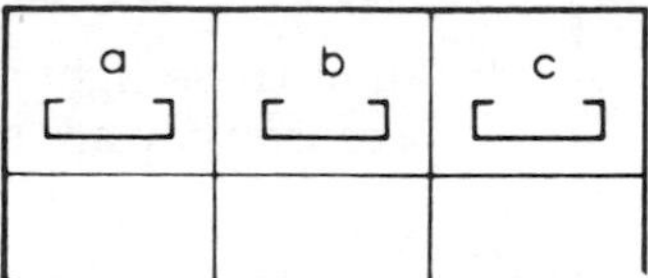

a	b	c

10. State what is meant by a weather-struck joint.

____

____

11. Describe how walling should be treated when it is finished.

____

____

5 Blockwork

Blocks

The use of blockwork has increased over the years because of the cheaper handling costs than brickwork, but the finish that is obtained is nowhere near as pleasing to the eye as that from face brickwork. The blocks tend to be drab in colour and the surface finish of some types of units is quite poor. There are far fewer joints in blockwork than in brickwork so it is very difficult to make adjustments in the joints to allow for differences in the dimensions of the blocks. If a block is laid and it does not quite meet the line, the weight of the block may also deter the craftsman from lifting it off the joint to re-lay it again. It therefore follows that a great deal of skill and patience is required to produce a good face in blockwork.

Types of blocks

Lightweight blocks. These are generally regarded as non load-bearing and may be produced from aerated concrete, which is concrete which has been treated with a powdered aluminium additive; this causes the concrete to expand rapidly, leaving it full of very small holes. These blocks are very light but are quite strong and have very good thermal insulating properties.

Other lightweight blocks are made by substituting alternative materials in place of the normal gravel used in dense concrete. These lightweight materials may be:

- *expanded clay,* which is clay that has been subjected to high temperature, expanded and formed into hard porous nodules. These are graded into different sizes as for aggregates.
- *fly ash,* which is a residue from furnaces, shown in Figure 5.1.
- *exfoliated mica,* such as vermiculite, which has been subjected to high temperatures, a process which releases the layers to form granules which are graded into aggregate sizes. These, when mixed with cement, form a very lightweight block.

All of these lightweight blocks have good thermal insulation. However, because they are so light they are not very good for sound insulation.

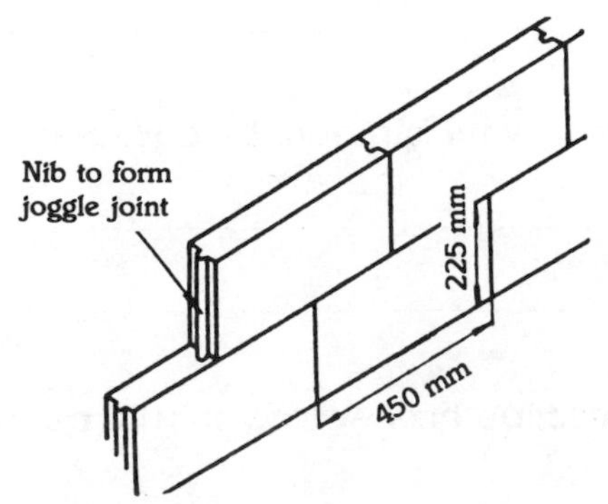

Figure 5.1 Fly ash block partition

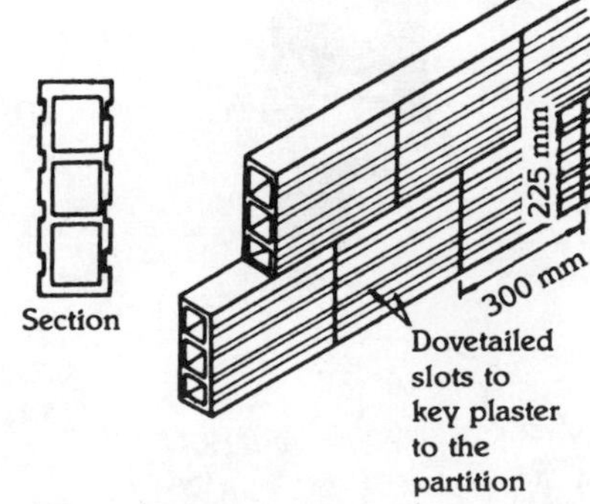

Figure 5.2 Hollow terra-cotta block partition

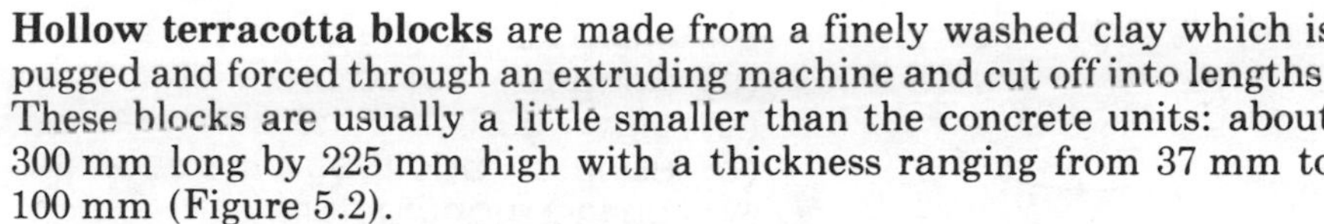
Hollow terracotta blocks are made from a finely washed clay which is pugged and forced through an extruding machine and cut off into lengths. These blocks are usually a little smaller than the concrete units: about 300 mm long by 225 mm high with a thickness ranging from 37 mm to 100 mm (Figure 5.2).

Dense concrete blocks are made with ordinary concrete and may be classified as load-bearing units. They are not so good for heat insulation because they are so dense, but are reasonably good for sound insulation in relation to their thickness.

Stacking

Because the blocks are so thin they are vulnerable to breakages if stacked carelessly. Most deliveries are now made on pallets, with the blocks being bound with iron strapping and covered with polythene sheets. They should be kept like this on site until they are required for use. When the strapping is released the blocks require planned removal from the stack, otherwise loose blocks at the end of the stacked rows will fall and break. A little thought and care can prevent a great deal of unnecessary wastage.

All blocks should be protected against the elements to prevent them from becoming saturated because:

- if they are subjected to freezing they are likely to become badly damaged.
- wet blocks become very heavy.
- some lightweight blocks are liable to deteriorate quite seriously due to being saturated.
- when the saturated blocks dry out they will shrink. This *moisture movement* is called *drying shrinkage,* which can cause serious cracking in a wall.

Heavy blocks are cumbersome to handle: lifters similar to those described in Chapter 1 may be used to great advantage when transporting them from the stack to the working place.

The methods of stacking the blocks and placing the spot boards are similar to those already described for bricks. When stacking the blocks on raised platforms it is essential that the platform is not overloaded.

Mortar for blockwork

The mortar for general blockwork may be composed of Portland cement/lime/sand mix in a ratio of 1 : 1 : 6.

For load-bearing walling, or for special purposes using dense blocks, a mix composed of 1 part Portland cement or rapid-hardening cement to 4 parts of sand or fine aggregate may be used.

Questions for you

1. The best way to prevent sound from travelling across a wall is to:
(a) build it with lightweight blocks
(b) render it with plaster
(c) build it with dense concrete blocks

a	b	c
[ ]	[ ]	[ ]

2. Aerated concrete blocks are made by:
(a) using powdered aluminium in the concrete
(b) blowing air into the concrete
(c) using an additive to increase the workability of the concrete during manufacture

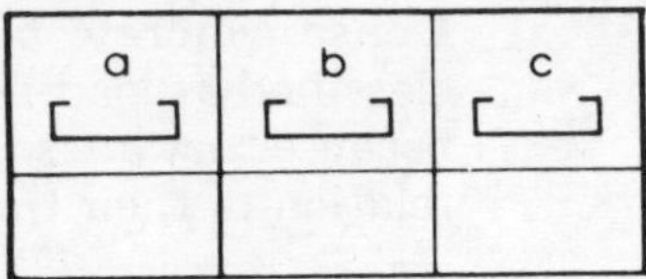

3. Moisture movement in blocks is:
(a) the process of becoming wet
(b) the process of becoming dry
(c) the expansion and contraction of the blocks

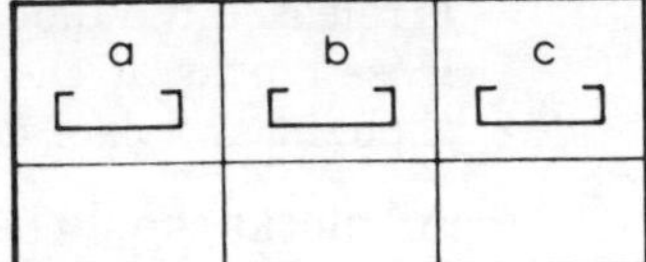

4. For general blockwork a suitable mortar mix would be:
(a) 1:2:8 cement/lime/sand
(b) 1:1:8 cement/lime/sand
(c) 1:1:6 cement/lime/sand

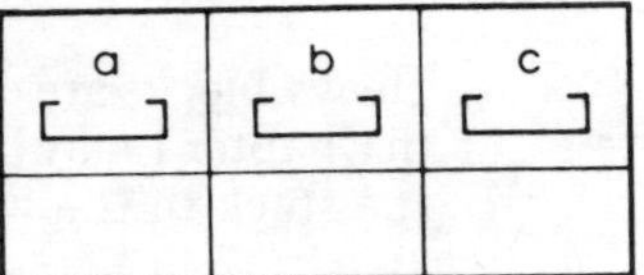

Building blockwork

The method of building with blocks is very similar to building with bricks. Figure 5.3 illustrates the building of straight walls in blockwork. The bond should be carefully set out at the base of the wall before bedding the blocks in mortar. So far as is possible, broken bonds should never be placed in the centre of the wall since not only are they unsightly but they may also create a weakness in the wall itself (Figure 5.4). If a wall length is such that a broken bond cannot be avoided then it is better to let it occur at an internal angle, as shown in Figure 5.5.

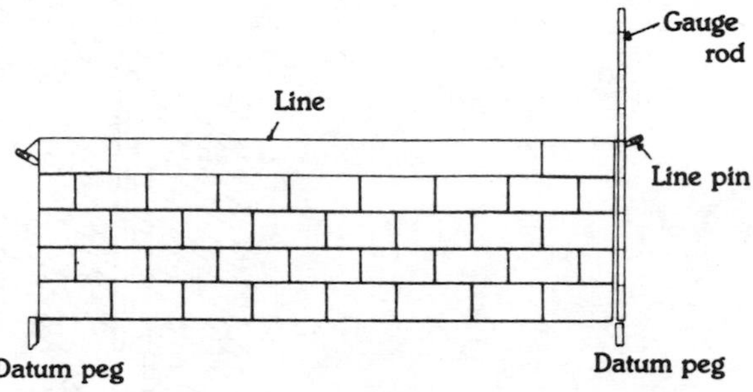

Figure 5.3 Method of building with blockwork

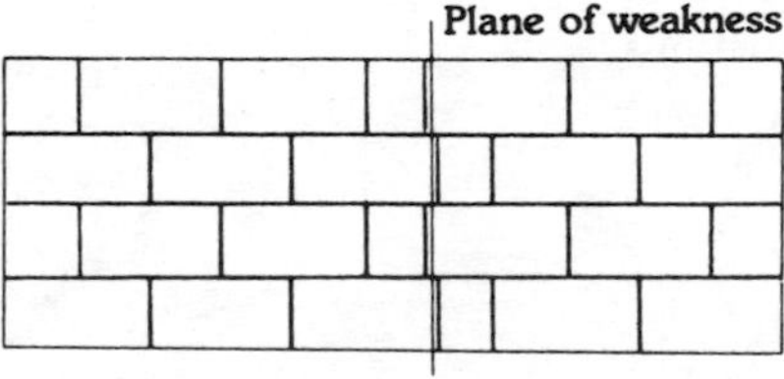

Figure 5.4 A broken bond which has been badly set out can often be avoided by setting out the bond 'dry' first

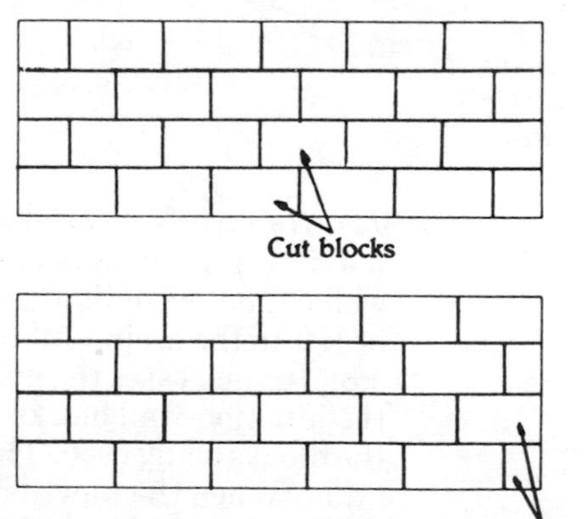

Figure 5.5 Alternative arrangements showing how to avoid broken bonds of less than half-block size

Cutting a block so that a good cut is shown on both sides of the block is also very difficult, and many manufacturers supply special units such as half and three-quarter lengths. Some of these are shown in Figure 5.12, p. 69.

Building partitions and junction walls

As *block partitions* are very thin, ranging from 50 mm to 100 mm, great care must be taken to ensure that they are well bonded at angles and intersections. The pinning up to the underside of ceilings should be solid so that the maximum amount of stability may be achieved. The partitions should not normally exceed three metres in height.

When building these thin partitions it is a good practice, wherever possible, to provide extra support by erecting profiles of 75 mm by 50 mm timbers and wedging them between floor and ceiling with folding wedges, as shown in Figure 5.6. Where the partition walls are attached to a main wall they should be block-bonded to gain the maximum stability (Figure 5.7).

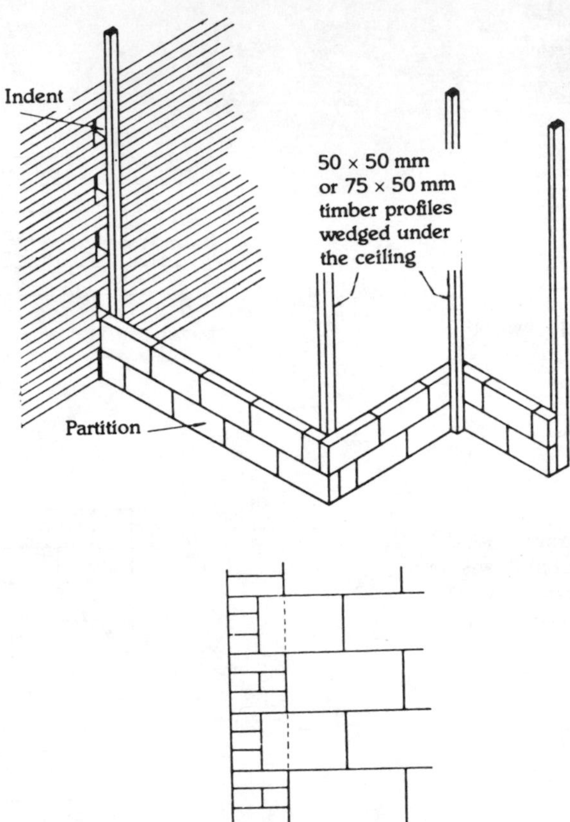

Figure 5.6 Method of placing profiles for partitions

Figure 5.7 Section showing the block-bonding of a partition into a main wall

Junction walls must also be well tied-in to the main walling to gain the maximum stability between the two walls. If, for some reason, the junction wall cannot be built at the same time as the main wall, then indents must be left in the main wall to receive the junction wall at a later stage (Figure 5.8). In such cases the indents must be wide enough to permit easy entry of the junction-wall blocks, and should therefore be about 25 mm wider than the blocks being used. The indents must be kept perfectly plumb with each other. When the junction-wall blocks are being laid care must be taken to ensure that the blocks being tied-in to the main wall are properly bedded into place and the joints well filled.

The same principle applies to the erection of partition walls, but in certain cases it may be permissible to insert reinforcing mesh into the main wall and along the partition wall, usually every other course. This will tie the two walls together without having to resort to excessive cutting at the internal angle (Figure 5.9).

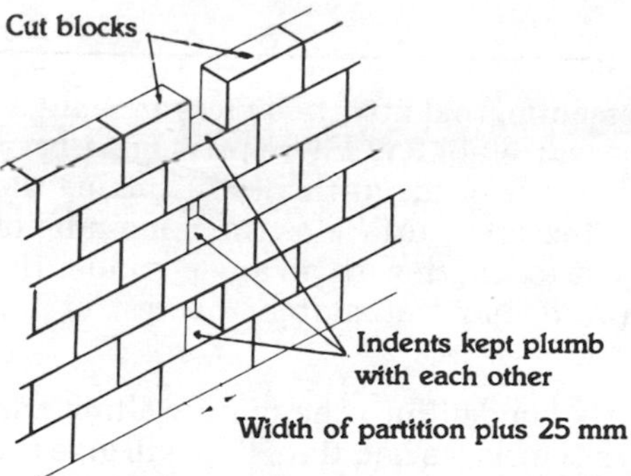

Figure 5.8 Method of providing bonding for a partition

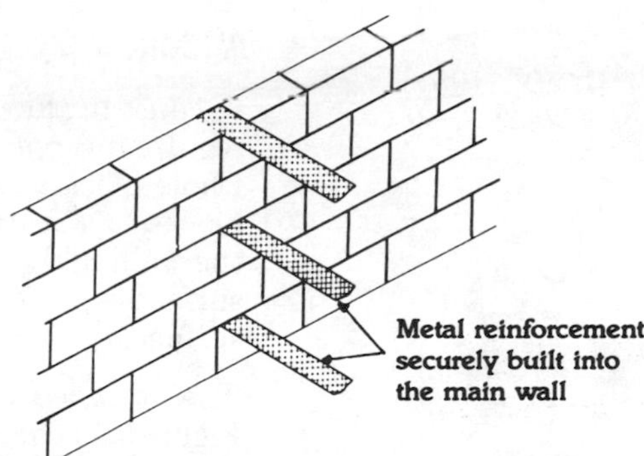

Figure 5.9 An alternative method of tying-in a partition

Quoins

There are several ways of building a quoin in blockwork:

- Figure 5.10 shows a good method of bonding a quoin in blockwork by cutting the corner block on each course.
- Figure 5.11 shows a method using either quarter units cut by hand or special units supplied by the manufacturer, some of which are detailed in Figure 5.12.
- Special corner units may be used (Figure 5.13).

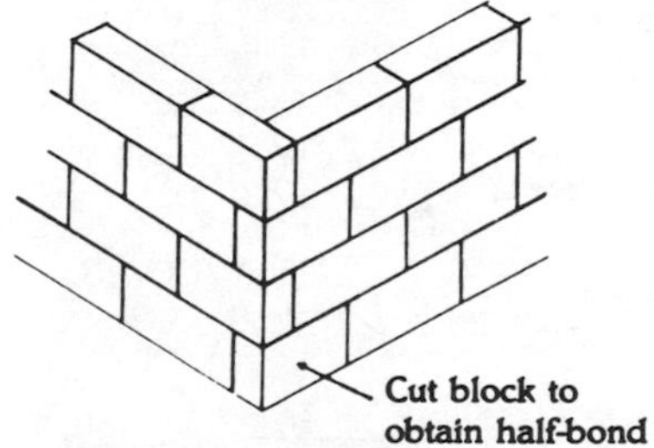

Figure 5.10 Method of building a quoin with 100 mm blocks

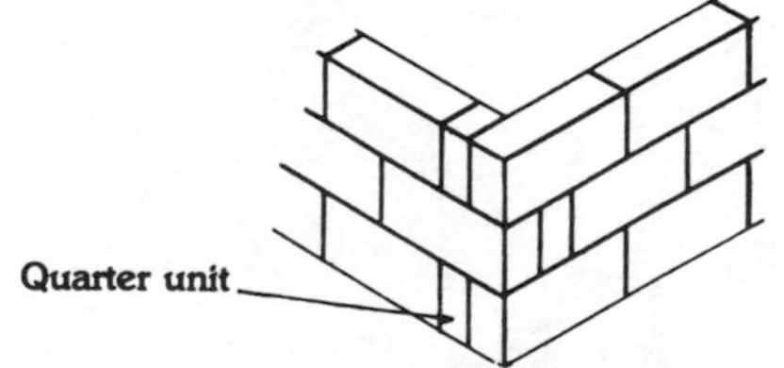

Figure 5.11 Building a quoin using quarter units

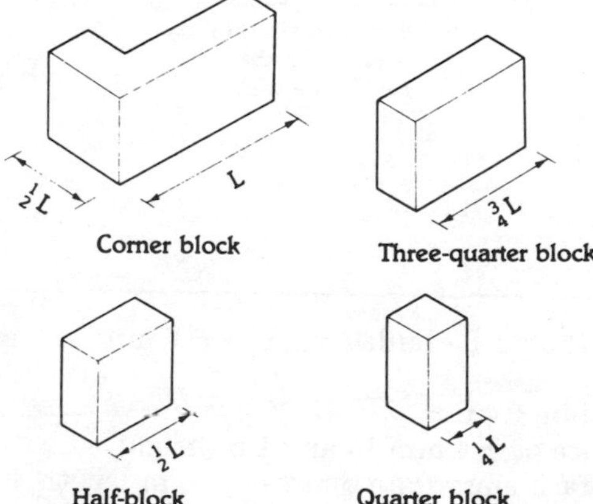

Figure 5.12 Special blocks

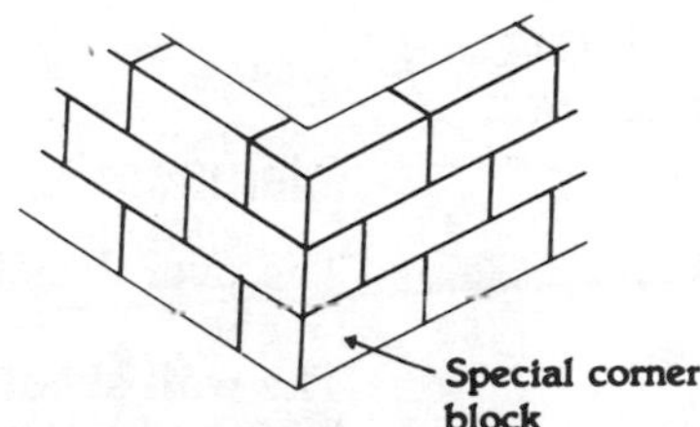

Figure 5.13 Building a quoin using special corner units

Attached piers

Because the blocks are so thin it is essential that attached piers are built at regular intervals in order to give the wall stability. These piers must be of whole-block or special-block size, because of the difficulty in cutting the blocks to size and leaving the same textured surface as the remainder of the walling. Even if the blocks are cut to length with an angle grinder the surface will then become smooth and may not match the rest of the surface.

The attached piers must be properly bonded into the main walling and Figure 5.14 shows a pier bonded with the blocks laid flat. This will give the narrowest attached pier. Figure 5.15 shows the method of bonding a pier if the depth can be increased to block size.

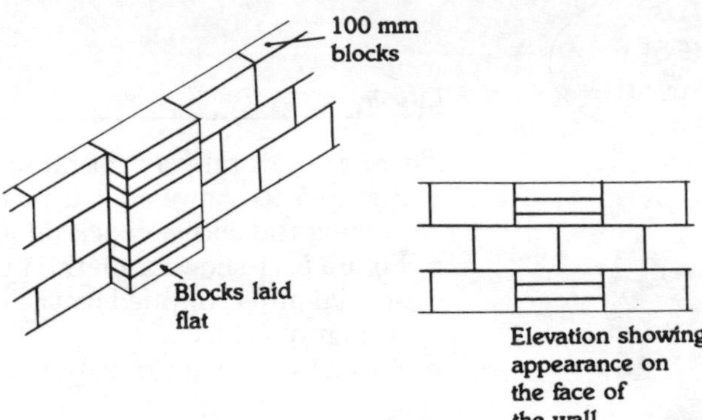

Figure 5.14 Bonding an attached pier into a main wall

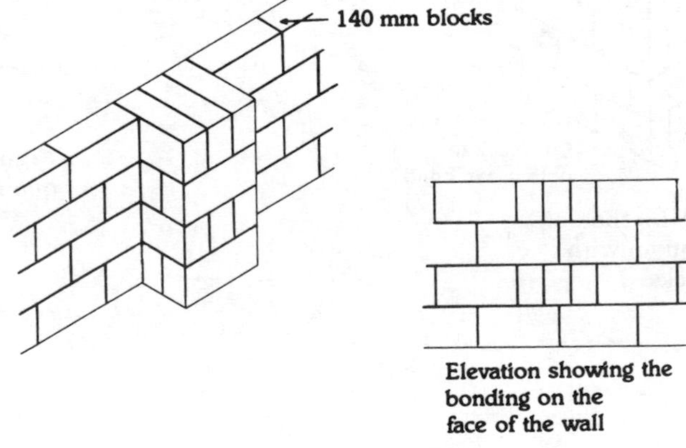

Figure 5.15 Bonding a buttressing pier into a main wall

Tolerances

The overall height of the wall should be built to gauge ± 6 mm in 3 m height.
The wall should be level to within ± 4 mm.
It should be plumb to a tolerance of ± 4 mm in any 1 m height.
It should not deviate along its face more than 5 mm in a 3 m length.
The thickness of the perpends should be 10 mm ± 3 mm, with a permitted deviation of verticality of 5 mm.

Estimating

To estimate the number of blocks in block walling measure the overall area and divide by the area of one block.

For example, if the total area of walling to be built is 150 square metres and the nominal face of a block is 450 mm by 225 mm, then the number of blocks required is as follows:

Area of one block $= 0.450 \text{ m} \times 0.225 \text{ m} = 0.10125 \text{ m}^2$

The number of blocks needed $= \dfrac{150}{0.10125}$

$= 1482$ (to the nearest block)

To this should be added a percentage to allow for wastage, say 2%.

Then the number of blocks required is $1482 + 30$

$= 1512$

Questions for you

5. Explain why it is so important to set out the bonding at the base of a wall to be built with blocks before actual building commences.

6. State where a cut block should be placed if it is necessary to have one.

7. Show with a sketch how to bond an attached pier into a block wall.

8. Describe the methods which may be used to tie a partition wall into a main wall in blockwork.

9. Describe the special units available from the manufacturer and explain their uses.

Openings in blockwork

Openings in blockwork are formed in the same manner as for brick walling. The bond should be carefully set out at the base of the wall so as to avoid difficult cutting at the reveals when the opening is being formed. If the opening is in cavity walling then special care must be taken when sealing the cavity; see Chapter 6. However, in order to avoid difficult cutting at the reveal it is possible to use specially made units for this work.

Openings may be bridged with reinforced concrete lintels, but the height of these lintels should be in line with the courses in the general walling, otherwise it would be necessary to cut blocks over the top of the lintel (Figure 5.16). The texture of the lintel should match the surrounding blockwork. An alternative method would be to use a steel lintel (see Chapter 2, Figure 2.55) and build the blocks over the opening.

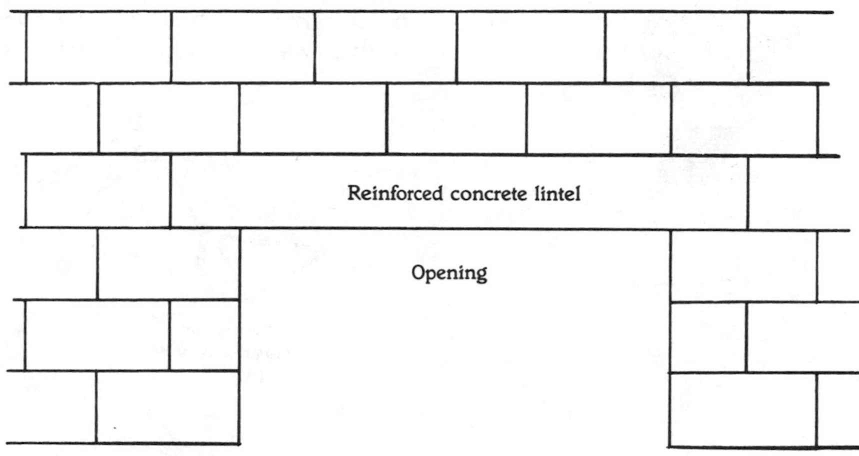

Figure 5.16 A reinforced concrete lintel in position

Tolerances

The lintel should be level ± 2 mm.
It should have a uniform bearing ± 10 mm.
Its horizontal position should be uniform ± 3 mm.
The opening should be in the position and to the size specified.
The reveals should be plumb ± 4 mm in 1 m height.

Questions for you

10. Describe how the reveal may be finished off at a window opening in a cavity wall built with blocks.

11. Describe the special care which must be taken if reinforced concrete lintels are to be placed over an opening.

6 Cavity walls

Cavity walling

Chapter 2 dealt with the construction of solid walls, that is, walls having one thickness only. This chapter describes the general construction of cavity walls, which are comprised of two separate walls, referred to as *leaves,* with a space in between. This space should not be less than 50 mm wide and has two advantages:

- It prevents rainwater passing from the outer leaf to the inner leaf, thus keeping the interior of the building dry.
- It forms a barrier to the loss of heat from the building, thus keeping the building warmer than one which is built with solid walling.

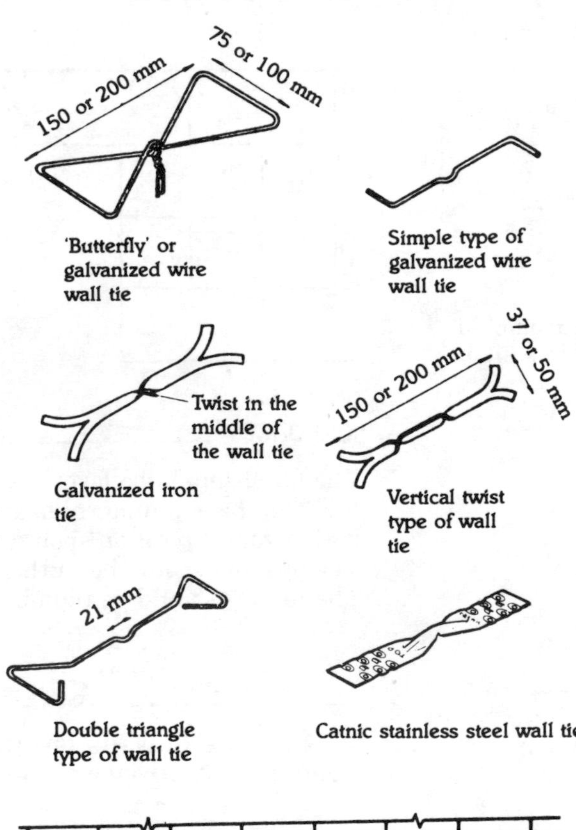

Figure 6.1 Cavity wall ties

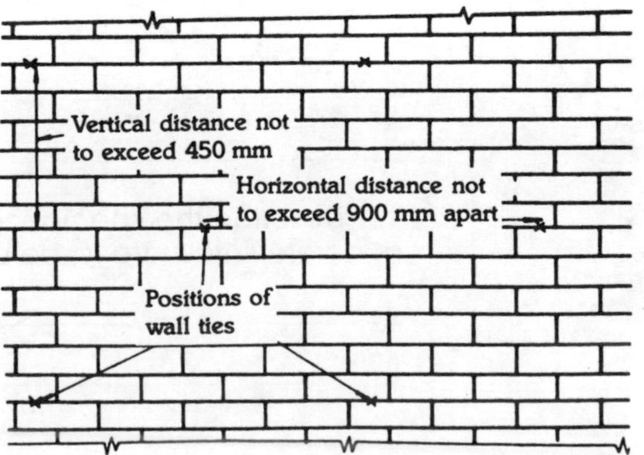

Figure 6.2 Elevation of a cavity wall showing the wall ties 'staggered' throughout the wall

If the cavity wall is built with two half-brick leaves, then for general purposes this may be regarded as having the same stability as a one-brick solid wall, provided that the two leaves are properly tied together. This is achieved by building in *wall ties* (Figure 6.1) at intervals not greater than 900 mm horizontally and 450 mm vertically and staggered, as shown in Figure 6.2, throughout the wall. These wall ties are so constructed as to prevent the passage of water across them and are made from galvanised iron or wire, or other suitable non-ferrous material. The cavity must be kept completely clear of mortar droppings or any other material in order to prevent water from travelling across and causing the interior wall to become damp. If the cavity is bridged, such as at reveals, then a *vertical damp-proof course* must be built into the wall (Figure 6.3).

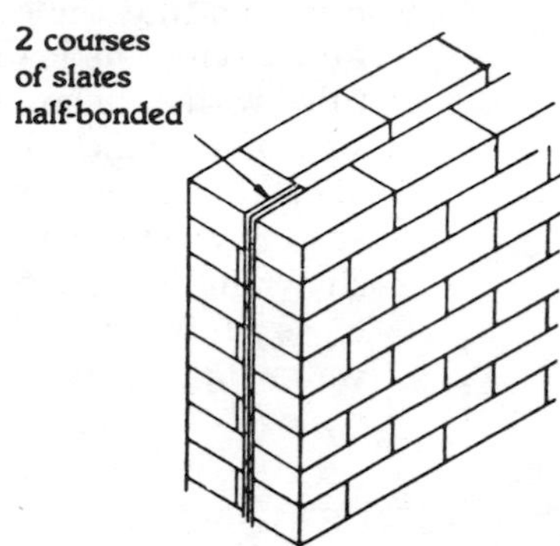

Figure 6.3 Sealing a cavity with a vertical damp-proof course

Cavity battens

When building a cavity wall the cavity is kept clean by means of *cavity battens* which are placed on the wall ties. The batten is raised by means of the wires which are attached, cleaned off, and then placed on the next layer of wall ties, and so on until the wall is completed (Figure 6.4). Even

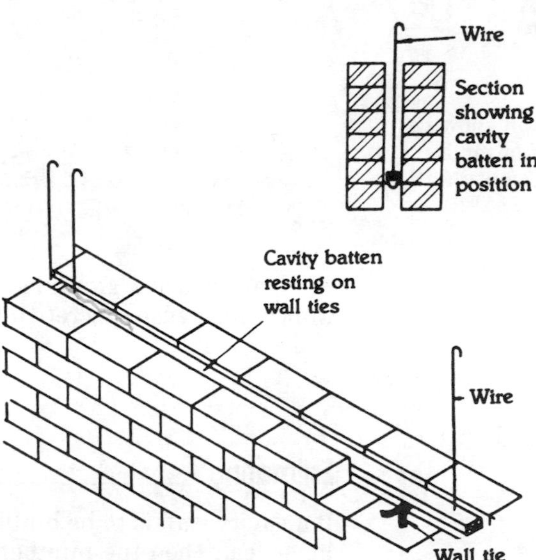

Figure 6.4 Method of keeping a cavity clean during construction

the use of cavity battens will not prevent some mortar droppings from falling down the cavity during building, so it is usual to provide *coring holes* at the bottom of the cavity by leaving bricks out of the first course approximately every metre along the wall in order to rake out any debris which might have fallen into the cavity. These holes are filled in when the work is completed.

Weepholes

It is also good practice to provide *weepholes* at intervals along the first course and also immediately above damp-proof courses which may be placed at cills and window heads. These holes are cross joints which have been left open to allow any moisture which may fall into the cavity to escape through the outer leaf.

Foundations

Cavity walls for housing may be built directly off the foundation concrete, provided that the ground immediately below the foundations is suitable for carrying the load of the building. In these cases the cavity is usually filled with a concrete of Portland cement and fine aggregate not exceeding 10 mm in a mix of 1 : 6. The filling is taken up to ground level and finished off with a steep slope falling towards the outer leaf at the top. This will shed any water, which may fall into the cavity, away from the inner leaf, as shown in Figure 6.5. Weepholes should be left in the outer leaf by leaving cross joints empty at metre intervals along this slope, or fillet, so that the water may escape.

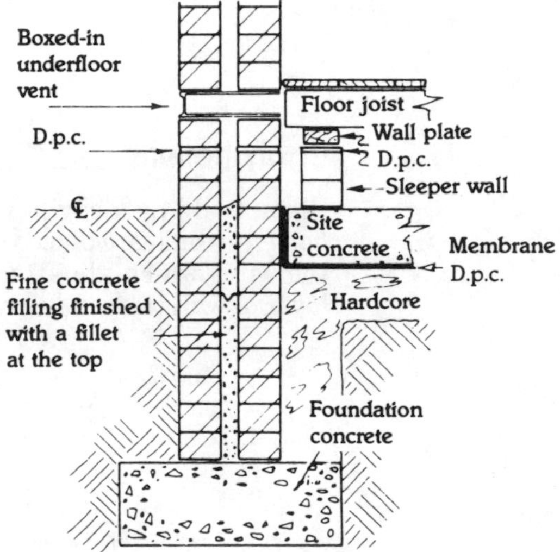

Figure 6.5 Section showing method of constructing a foundation for a cavity wall

The walling below ground level may be constructed in brickwork or blockwork using dense concrete blocks, built with a cement/sand mortar mix of 1 : 4.

Estimating

If a cavity wall is to be built of bricks on the outer leaf and blocks on the inner leaf, then the number of units required to construct such walling would be calculated by measuring the wall overall and dividing by the number of bricks in 0.84 square metres. This, in stretcher bond, may be assumed to be 48 and the nominal area of the blocks, say, 450 mm by 225 mm. The method of estimating the amount of walling is to measure the length and height of the wall overall, ignoring openings, then deduct the sizes of the openings from the total. Figure 6.6 illustrates this quite clearly.

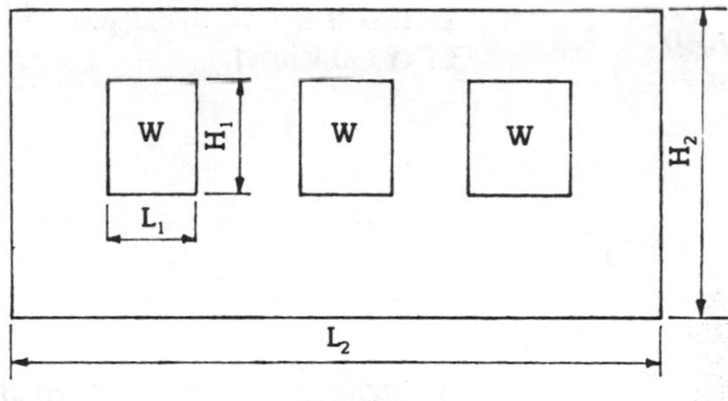

Figure 6.6 Diagram showing the method of calculating the area of a wall

The length L_2 is multiplied by the height H_2 and the total area of the three windows, each L_1 multiplied by H_1, is deducted.

Example

If the total area of a cavity wall to be built is 200 square metres and the bricks laid at 48 to 0.84 square metres and the nominal size of the blocks is 450 mm by 225 mm, calculate the total number of units required.

$$\textit{Bricks} \quad \frac{200 \times 48}{0.84} = 11428.5$$

$$\textit{Blocks} \quad \frac{200}{0.45 \times 0.225} = 1975.3$$

Additional units, say 2% of each total, should be added to allow for wastage.

Tolerances

The overall height of the wall should be built to gauge ± 5 mm and with regular joint thickness.
The wall should be level within a tolerance of ± 4 mm in 2 m length.
The walling should be plumb within a tolerance of ± 3 mm in any 1 m height.
There should be no face plane deviation more than 6 mm in a 3 m length.
The horizontal d.p.c. should be positioned at a minimum of 150 mm above the finished ground level and flush to the wall plus 2 mm.
Airbricks, cavity liners and d.p.c. trays should be positioned as indicated on the drawings.
Positions of cavity insulators, ties and slab/batts should conform to manufacturer's instructions.
The vertical d.p.c. at reveals should be flush with the reveal plus 25 mm.
The permitted deviation for perpends should not exceed 5 mm.

Questions for you

1. State what is meant by the term 'cavity wall'.

2. List the advantages of having cavity walls as the external walls of a building.

3. State the minimum width of the cavity.

4. Describe how the two leaves of a cavity wall are stabilised.

5. Describe how a cavity is kept clean during building operations.

Openings in cavity walls

Figure 6.7 shows two methods of sealing the cavity at a reveal when the brickwork is built with stretcher bond. In such cases the headers are made up from bats. As the outer leaf of the cavity wall is only a half brick in thickness then any unit shown as a header must be a half bat. (This is one of the occasions when the use of the closer or half-bat gauge, mentioned in Chapter 1, would be invaluable.) Sometimes the outer leaf of the cavity may be built with a Flemish or English bond for decorative reasons. This method would be particularly useful where an extension is being added to a building and the bonding of the new work is required to match the existing brickwork.

Where the inner leaf is to be built of blocks, the sealing of the cavity at a reveal is done by building up a straight joint with a d.p.c. and tying the two leaves together by building in wall ties at every 450 mm in height and not more than 300 mm from the reveal (Figure 6.8).

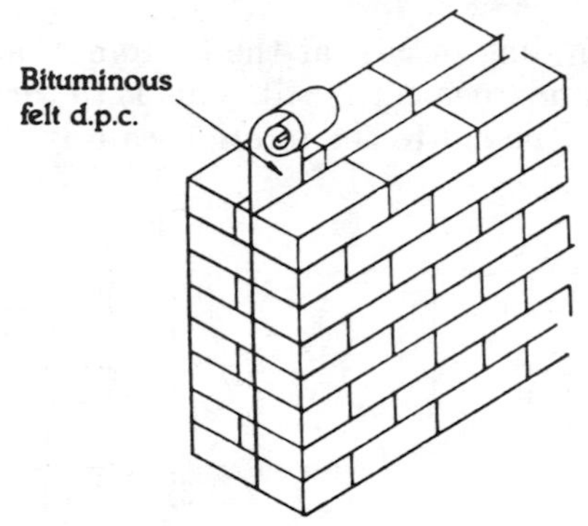

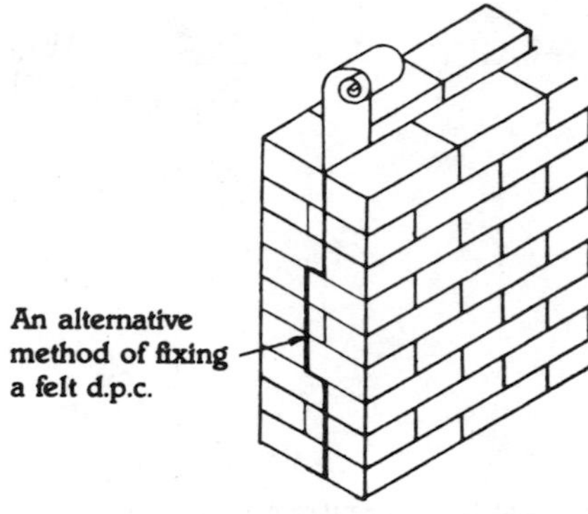

Figure 6.7 Methods of sealing cavities

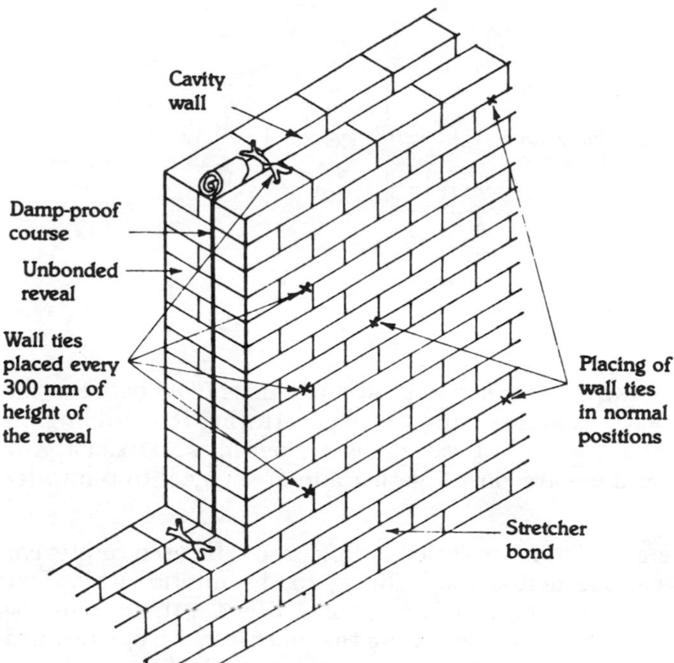

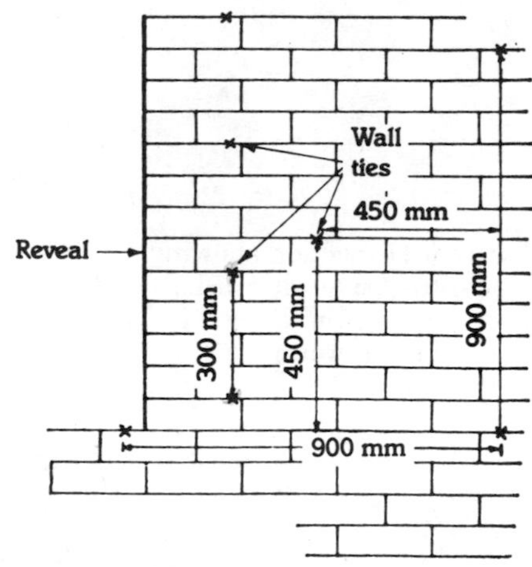

Figure 6.8 Placing of wall ties at an unbonded reveal in cavity walling

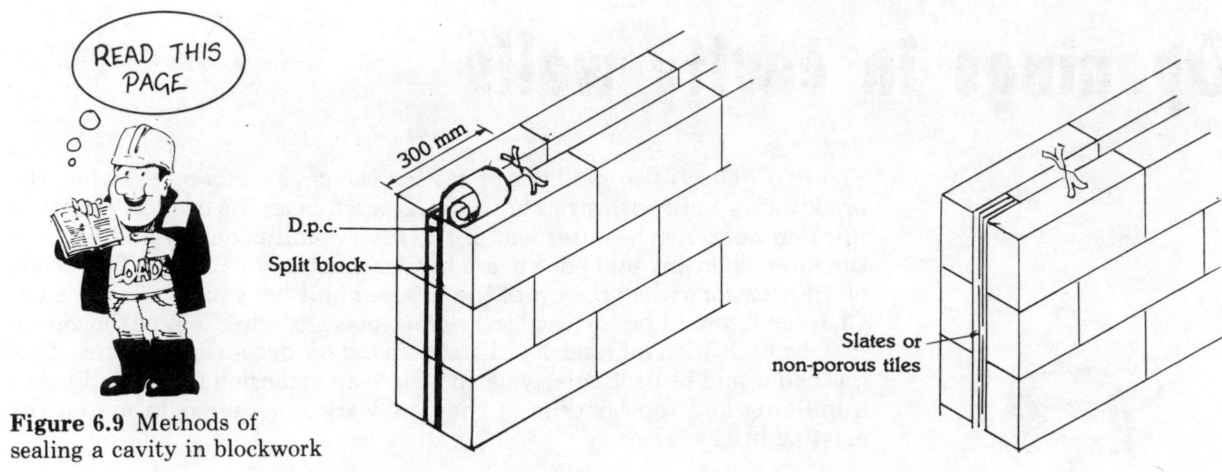

Figure 6.9 Methods of sealing a cavity in blockwork

Figure 6.9 shows a cavity wall which is built with blocks in both leaves. As the cavity is usually only 50 mm wide, a split block has to be used in order to seal the cavity at the reveal, as required under the Building Regulations.

When building-in cills at the bottom of an opening, a d.p.c. should be built-in underneath the cill. This is to throw off any water which might penetrate the cill to the interior walling (Figures 6.10, 6.11).

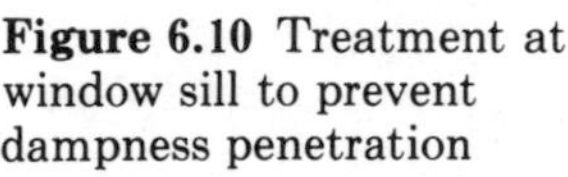

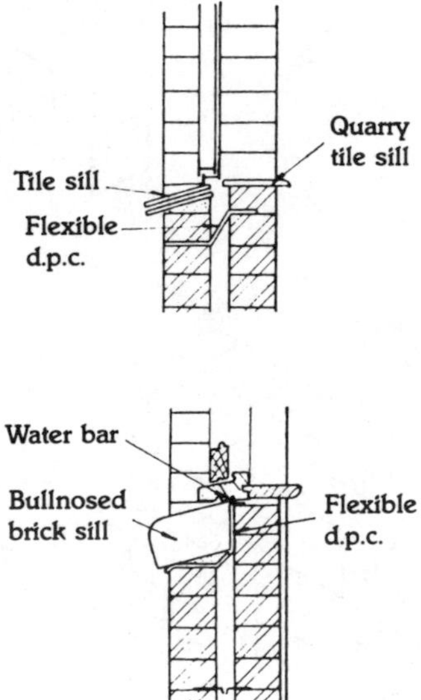

Figure 6.10 Treatment at window sill to prevent dampness penetration

Figure 6.11 Section showing typical treatment at a brick sill to prevent the penetration of water

Figure 6.11 also shows a *water bar* in position. This is fixed between the timber and brick cills to prevent any water penetrating the building. In general, to prevent the ingress of water, a water bar may be fixed at any point where two surfaces are close together and are subject to rainwater falling on them.

At any point where the cavity is sealed a d.p.c. must be used to prevent dampness from passing across the bridging to the interior wall. This principle applies to the bridging of an opening where a d.p.c. must be provided to throw off rainwater away from the inner leaf. An opening in a cavity wall may be bridged in one of a number of methods:

- by means of a reinforced concrete lintel which is often shaped in cross-section, as shown in Figure 6.12, by being greatly reduced on the front edge. This type of lintel is called a *boot lintel.*

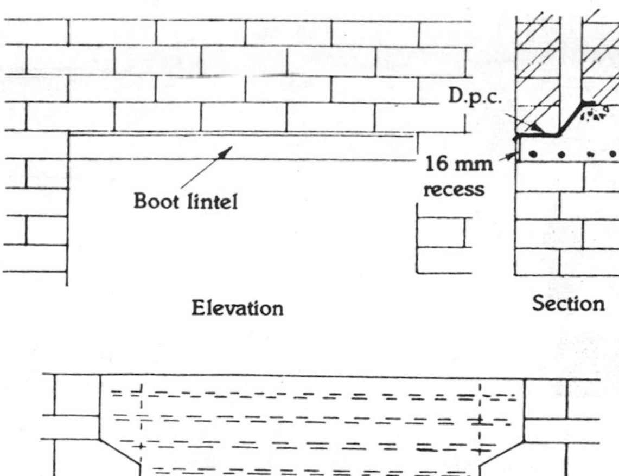

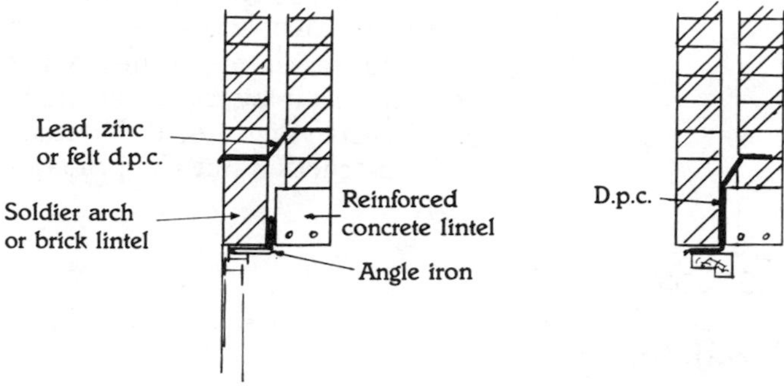

Figure 6.12 A 'boot' lintel

Figure 6.13 Treatment at window heads to prevent water penetration

- by using a normal reinforced concrete lintel on the inner leaf and a *brick lintel* or *soldier arch* on the outer leaf supported by an angle iron (Figure 6.13). A d.p.c. is placed across the wall above the lintel and arch, and sloped downwards to throw off any water towards the outer leaf.
- by using a *steel lintel.* There are a number of patent types of these available on the market but the same basic principles apply to each, in that they must be strong enough to carry the weight over the opening and they must direct the water away from the inner leaf. Typical shapes are shown in Figures 6.14, 6.15. L1/S and L1/HD are the manufacturer's code numbers for the lintels: L1/S is for standard work and L1/HD is for heavy duty work.

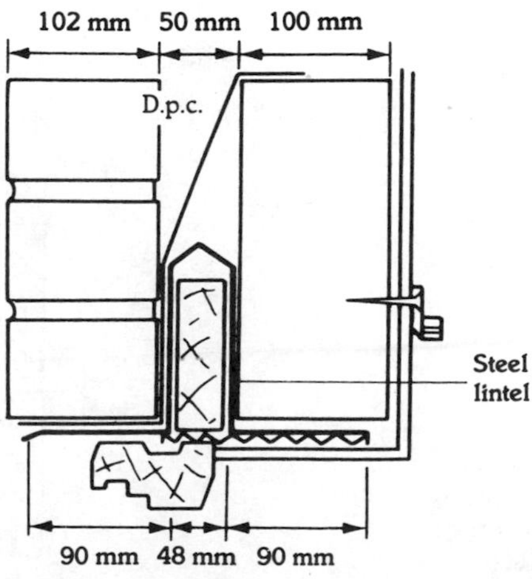

Figure 6.14 L1/S for 50 mm cavity wall construction

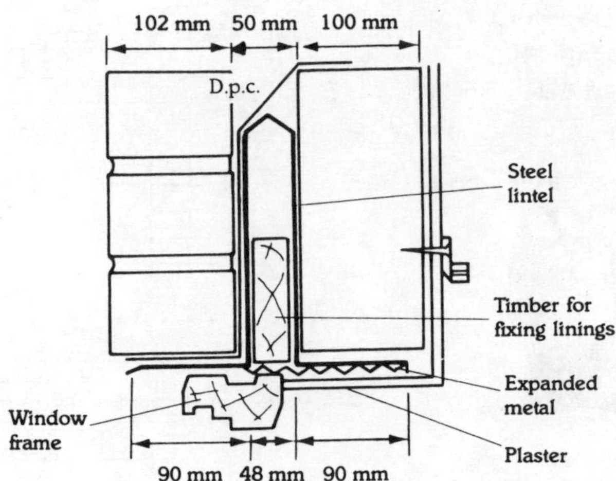

Figure 6.15 L1/HD for 50 mm cavity wall construction heavy-duty loading

If a reinforced concrete lintel is placed right across the width of the cavity wall over an opening then this will create a *cold bridge* and will affect the thermal insulation of the cavity at that position. It is, therefore, better to provide a gap by using a steel lintel in conjunction with the concrete unit, as shown in Figure 6.16. There are quite a number of variations of this form of construction but the principle in each case is the same.

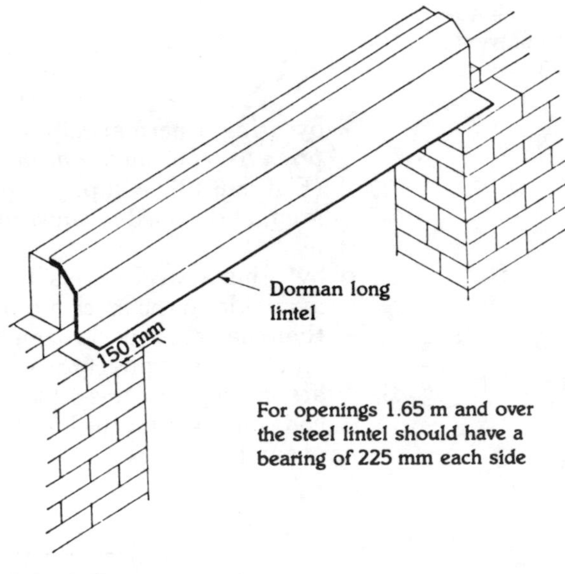

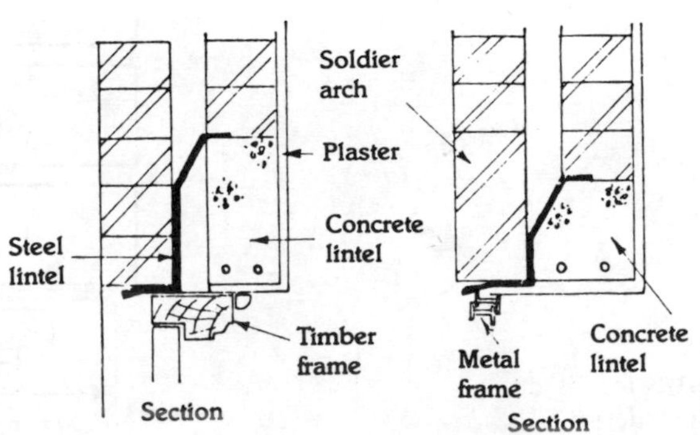

Figure 6.16 Alternative methods of bridging an opening showing different shapes of steel lintels

Tolerances

The lintel should be level ± 2 mm.
Its bearing should be uniform ± 10 mm.
Its horizontal position should be uniform ± 3 mm.

Fitting door and window frames

This is discussed in Chapter 3.

Thresholds

Thresholds are placed at the entrances of buildings. The bricks or tiles which are used for this work should be well burnt and capable of resisting hard wear as well as severe weather conditions. Engineering bricks and quarry tiles make excellent materials for this work. The bricks should be laid on a bed of concrete. The steps should be level with just a very small slope outwards, no more than 3 or 4 mm, to shed any water that falls on them. The steps should also be level across their width. All the steps should have equal risers as it is quite dangerous to have uneven heights of steps. Similarly, the treads must all have the same width. If there is no wall to which the steps can abut, then cramps must be built into the ends of the steps to prevent dislodgement, as shown in Figure 6.17.

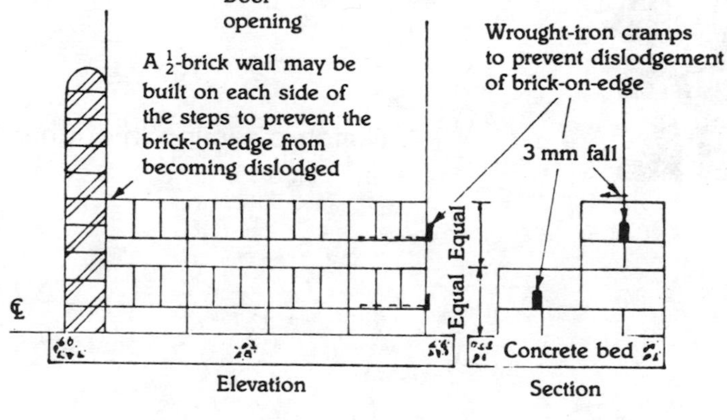

Figure 6.17 A simple straight flight of brick steps showing methods of preventing dislodgement of bricks on edge

Ventilators

There are instances where ventilators have to be built into a cavity, for example to allow air to pass through the wall to the underside of a timber floor, or to provide ventilation to a room, especially one containing a boiler. In such cases the ventilator should be *boxed-in* so that the air passes direct to the area which is to be ventilated. This may be effected by a metal cover or built up with slates or other similar material (Figure 6.18).

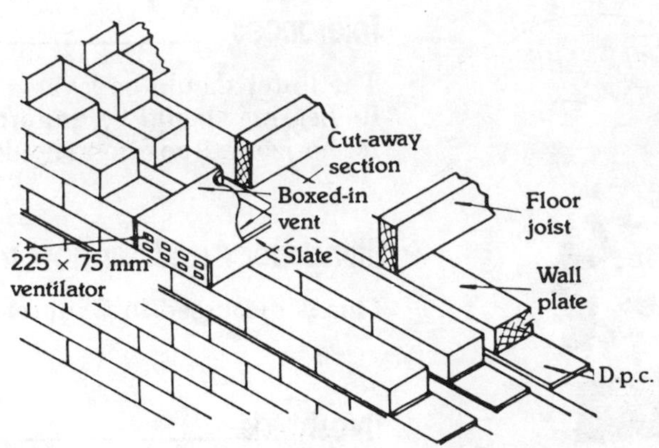

Figure 6.18 Method of 'boxing in' a ventilator

The ventilator may be bridged by using a slate or a 'Welsh Arch' as described in Chapter 2.

Questions for you

6. Describe how a reveal to a window opening is constructed.

7. Sketch a section through a typical window cill in a cavity wall.

8. Describe what is meant by the term 'boot lintel'.

9. A cold bridge is caused by:
(a) a solid concrete lintel over an opening
(b) a solid concrete floor
(c) the walling built over a ventilator

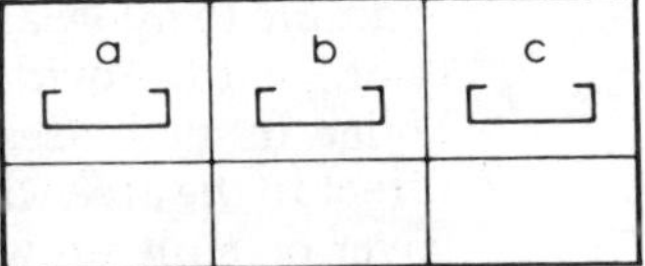

a	b	c
[ ]	[ ]	[ ]

Cavity insulation

The insulation value of a cavity is dependent upon the stillness of the air within it. As an illustration of this, blow across your hand and you will notice that it feels cool. This is because the moving air is extracting heat from the surface of the skin. The same effect is obtained by blowing across the surface of a hot liquid. Therefore, if the air inside the cavity is in motion then the leaves will remain cool. For good heat insulation it is usual to have non-ventilated cavities.

In order to increase the heat-insulating properties of a cavity it is good practice to place insulation slabs in the cavity. These insulation slabs are 50 mm thick and 450 mm in width and are laid on edge upon the wall ties (Figure 6.19). One method of fixing these into position is as follows:

1) The wall ties are placed into position across the cavity.
2) The cavity battens are placed upon the wall ties.
3) The two leaves are built up to the height of the next layer of wall ties.
4) The cavity battens are removed and the cavity thoroughly cleaned out.
5) The insulation slabs are lowered into the cavity so that they rest on the previous layer of wall ties.
6) When the cavity filling is complete the next layer of wall ties are placed across the cavity and the whole process repeated until the wall is complete.

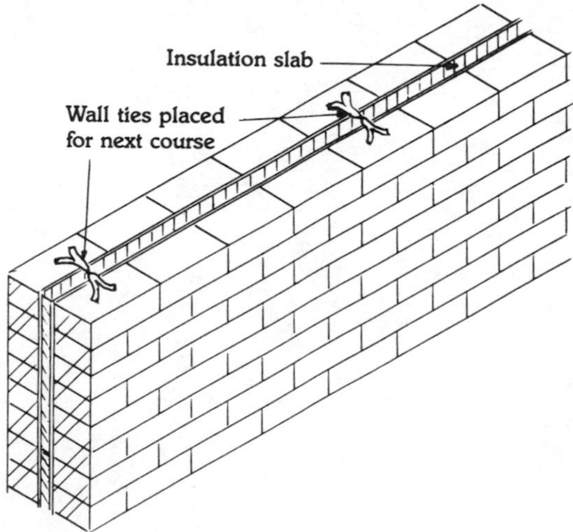

Figure 6.19 A cavity wall showing the application of insulation slabs

Note This sequence is for guidance only. The detail would vary according to the type of insulation material used. Always ensure that the manufacturer's instructions are obeyed.

Another excellent method of providing insulation in a cavity wall is by using special blocks which have an insulation slab fixed to one side of each block, as shown in Figure 6.20. The blocks are laid in the normal way with the insulation placed in the cavity. The insulating slab is approximately 35 mm wide and laid within the cavity so there is still a small gap between the slab and the outer leaf of the walling.

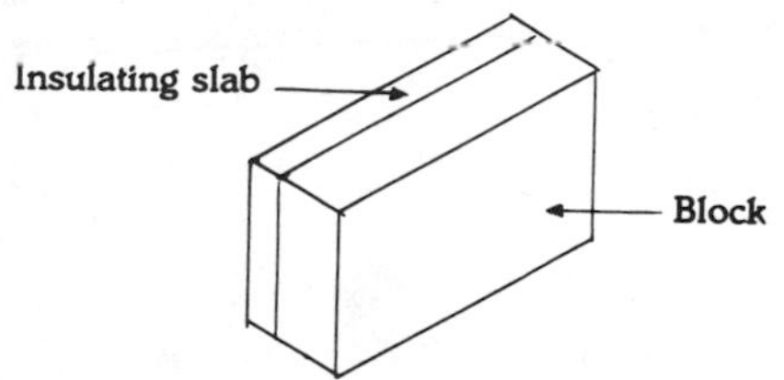

Figure 6.20 Special block with insulating slab attached

Questions for you

10. Describe the method of installing insulation slabs into a cavity.

11. Describe the method of providing ventilation to an underfloor area or to a room.

7 Chimney breasts, flues and stacks

Chimneys and flues

Definitions

The following definitions relate to the construction of chimneys, flue pipes, hearths and fireplace recesses.

A chimney is part of a structure of a building forming any part of a *flue.*

A flue is a passage for conveying the discharge of an appliance to the external air. It should be at least 175 mm in diameter.

A flue pipe is a pipe forming a flue, but does not include a pipe built as a lining into a chimney.

A Class I appliance is an open fire or a solid fuel or oil burning appliance having an output rating not exceeding 45 kW.

A Class II appliance is a gas appliance having an input rating not exceeding 45 kW.

A high-rating appliance is a solid fuel or oil burning appliance having, in either case, an output rating exceeding 45 kW or a gas appliance having an input rating exceeding 45 kW.

The materials used for the building of chimneys must:
- be of a non-combustible nature
- be of such a quality and thickness that they will not be adversely affected by heat.

The construction of chimneys must:
- be of such thickness as to prevent the ignition of any part of the structure.
- prevent any smoke or products of combustion escaping into the building.

Construction of hearths

Hearths in ground floors may be supported by fender walls (Figure 7.1). The top of the hearth must not finish below the floor level. If a sunken hearth is required, then at least 150 mm of the hearth must be level with the floor, as shown in Figure 7.2. In an upper floor the hearth may be formed by using reinforced concrete, as shown in Figure 7.3. If this hearth is being supported by the wall then it is important to remember that the slab is then a cantilevered unit, so the reinforcement must be placed at the upper part of the slab and not the bottom. Any timber which may be used for casting the concrete must be removed if it is within 250 mm of the upper surface of the hearth.

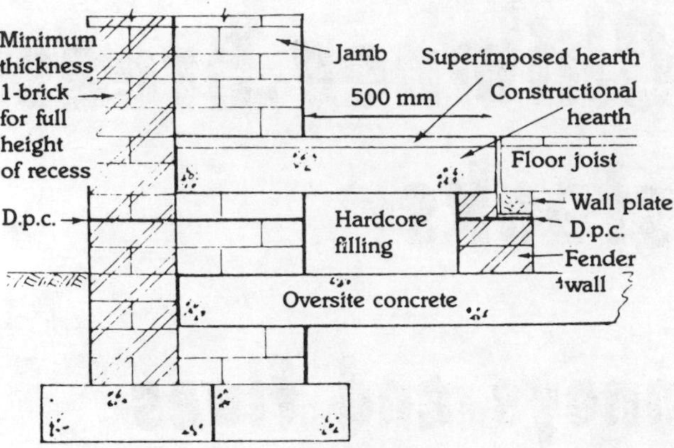

Figure 7.1 Section through a ground floor fireplace

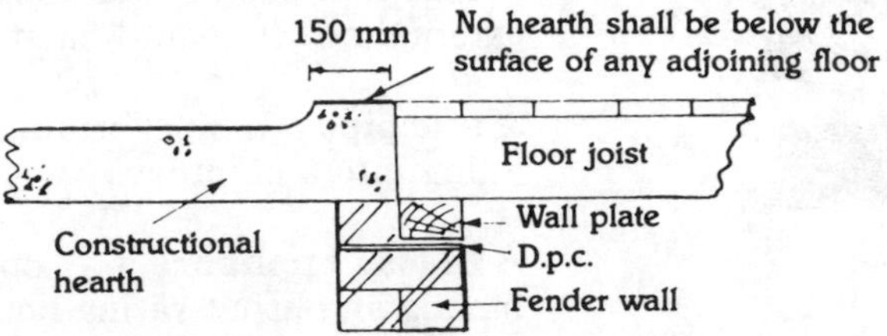

Figure 7.2 Section through a sunken hearth

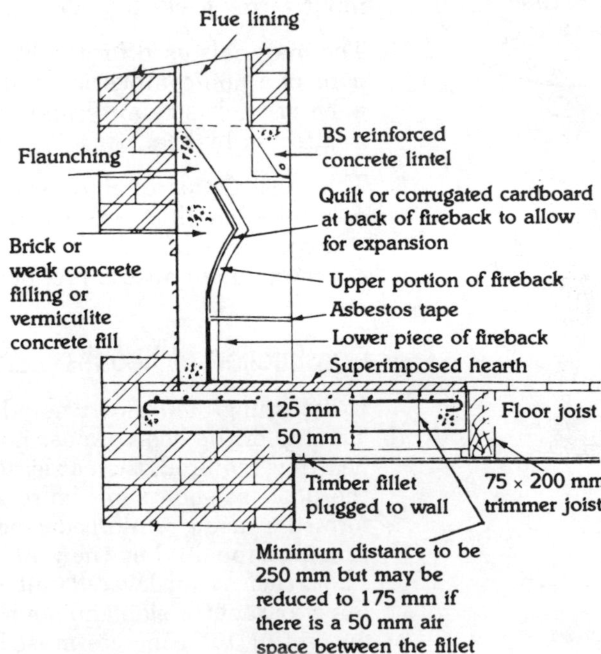

Figure 7.3 Section through an upper floor fireplace recess

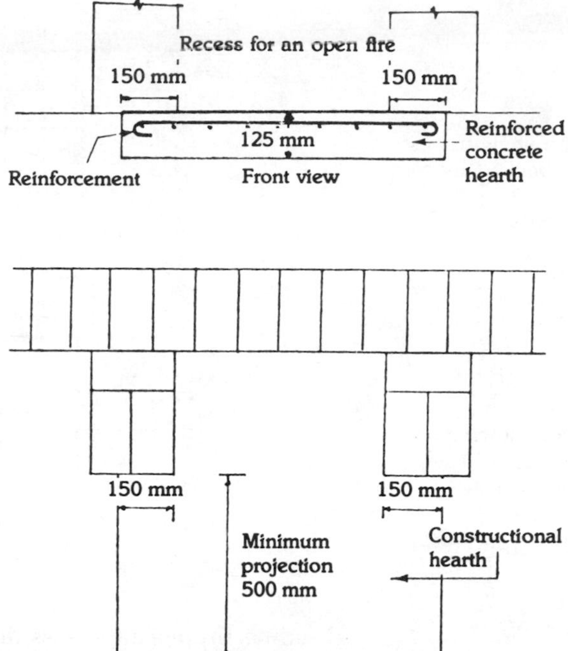

Figure 7.4 Minimum dimensions for a constructional hearth

For Class I appliances and open fires within a recess, it is necessary to provide a hearth in order to reduce the fire risk. This constructional hearth, shown in Figure 7.4, should be:

- not less than 125 mm thick.
- not lower than any floor built of combustible material.
- extended within the recess to the back and jambs of the recess and projected not less than 500 mm in front of the jambs and not less than 150 mm each side of the jambs.

Fireplace recesses

Fireplace recesses or chimney breasts must be well-bonded in order to avoid any possible movement which may allow cracking of the walling and thereby possibly letting smoke or fumes escape into the building. Figure 7.5 shows the bonding of a typical chimney breast into a one brick wall, and Figure 7.6 shows a similar recess built into a cavity wall.

If two fireplaces are back-to-back in the same building, then the back of the recess may be reduced to a half brick in thickness as shown in Figure 7.7. If the fireplaces are in separate buildings then the back must be not less than one brick in thickness, as shown in Figure 7.5.

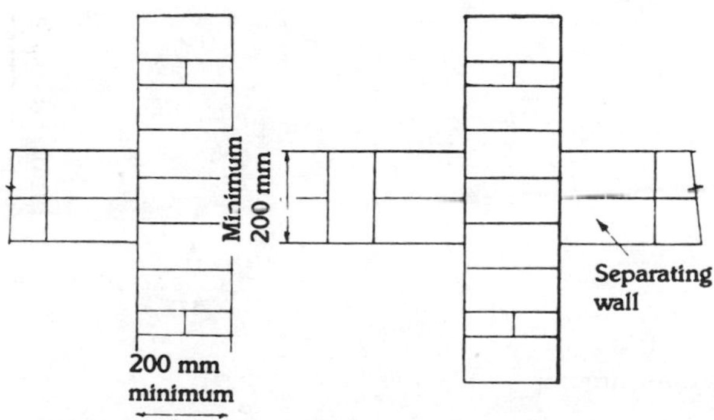

Figure 7.5 Plan showing the minimum thickness of the back of a fireplace in a 1-brick wall

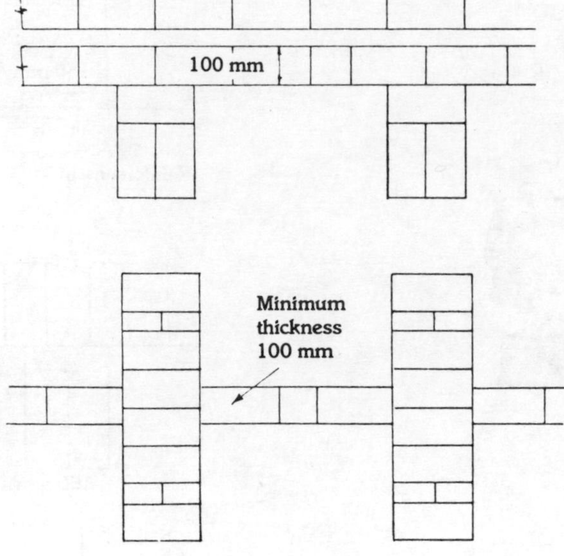

Figure 7.6 Plan showing a recess which is backed by a cavity wall

Figure 7.7 Plan showing the minimum thickness of the back of a fireplace recess in a wall other than a separating wall

Building fireplace recesses in blockwork is extremely uneconomical as it usually involves excessive cutting of blocks to achieve a bonding pattern and this results in quite a lot of wastage. It is, therefore, usually better to combine brick jambs with block-built walls.

The height of the opening should be 570 to 600 mm above the upper level of the hearth and may be bridged with a reinforced concrete lintel cast to the shape, as shown in Figure 7.8. This shows the positioning of the lintel and the gathering over of the flue. The flue lining should start immediately at the top of the fireplace opening.

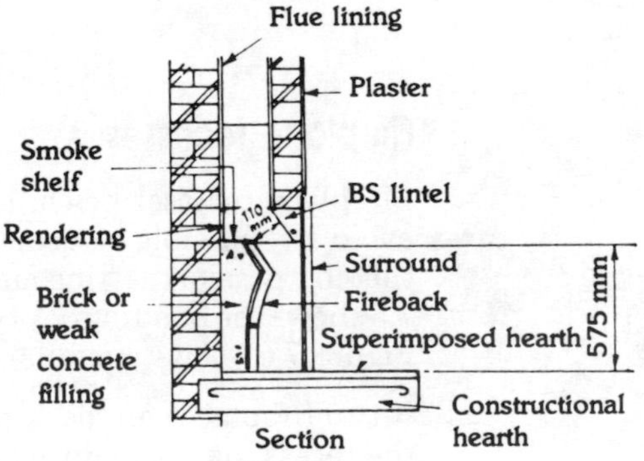

Figure 7.8 The positioning of a BS lintel in relation to an open fireplace

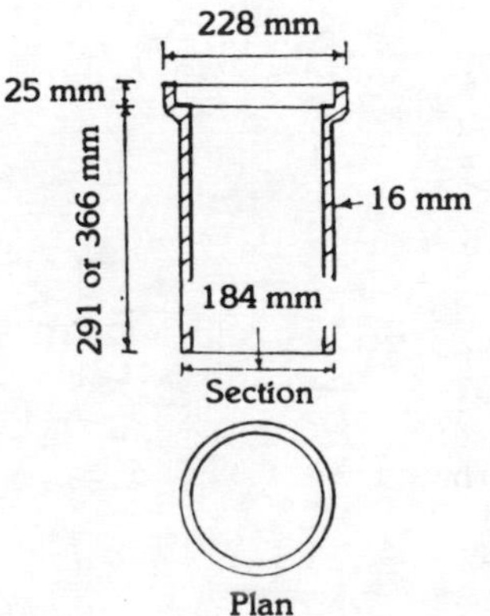

Figure 7.9 Section through a straight unit

Figure 7.10 Sections through curved units

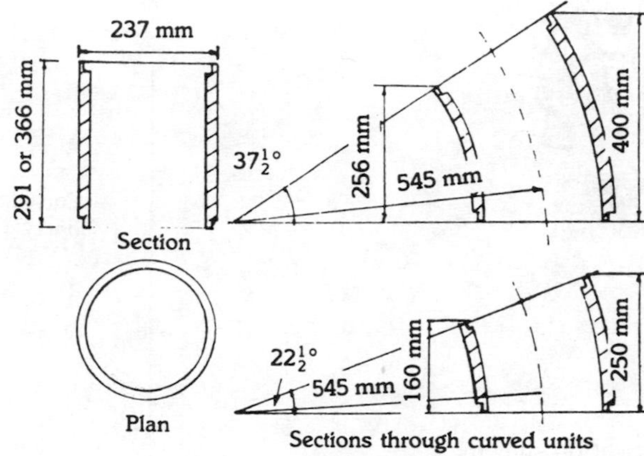

Figure 7.11 237 mm diameter rebated flue linings. Also available in 191 mm diameter units

Figure 7.12 Methods of checking accuracy of shapes of flue linings

Flues must be lined with any one of the following:

- rebated or socketed clay flue linings (Figures 7.9–7.11).
- Rebated or socketed flue linings made from kiln burnt aggregate and high alumina cement.
- Glazed vitrified clay pipes.
- Terracotta liners.

The methods of checking flue liners for accuracy are shown in Figure 7.12.

Flue linings should fit properly together. Figure 7.13 shows how the *spigot end* should sit inside the *socket.*

If a flue is required to *travel,* then its complete length must be lined using curved sections at each end of the travel, as shown in Figure 7.14.

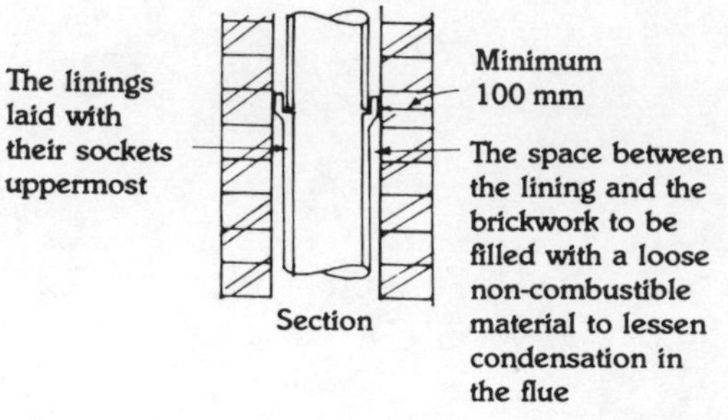

Figure 7.13 Section showing the method of building in linings and insulating them against excessive condensation

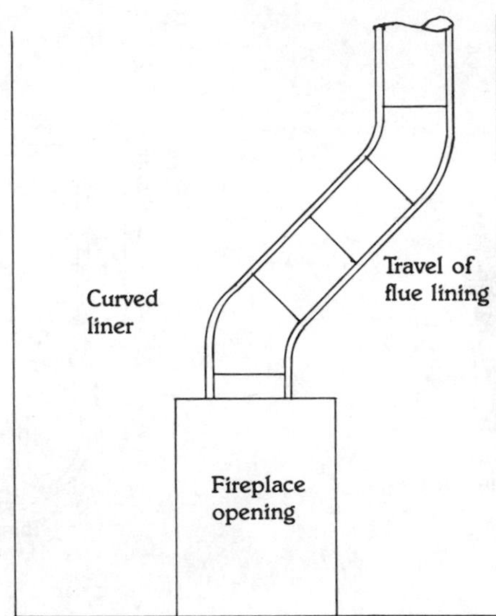

Figure 7.14 Section showing the travel of a flue and the lining

Fireclay is a refractory clay that will resist the effects of high temperature. It is usually mixed with water only and used for:

- sealing any gaps, for example where the flue pipe enters the flue or the joints in a firelump at the back of a fireplace. In fact, it is used anywhere which is subjected to heat.
- bedding firebricks which are also made from a refractory clay and are resistant to heat. These are used for lining large flues for industrial chimneys or for lining furnaces.

Tolerances

The gauge of the brickwork or blockwork for the chimney breast should match the adjoining walls.

The brickwork or blockwork should be level to match the adjoining wall.

The chimney breast should be plumb within a tolerance of ± 3 mm in 1 m height.

All d.p.c. should be correctly positioned and flush with the face of the wall + 2 mm. All joins and angles should have a minimum lap of 100 mm.

Questions for you

1. Define the term 'chimney'.

2. Define the term 'flue'.

3. Explain why special care must be taken when building chimneys.

4. Describe how a flue may be formed.

5. Draw **TWO** plans showing the bonding of alternate courses for a two-flue chimney stack.

6. The minimum thickness of a hearth used in conjunction with a class 1 appliance is:
(a) 100 mm
(b) 125 mm
(c) 150 mm

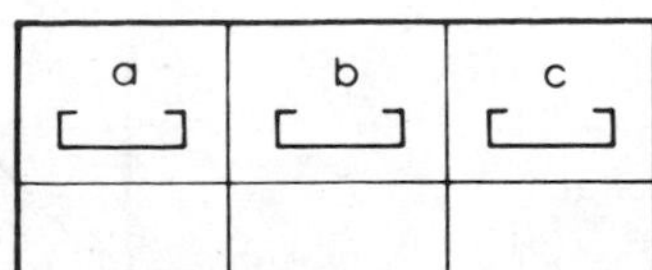

a	b	c

Chimney construction

This work should be done with great care, as the outer surface of the chimney is subjected to all types of severe weather conditions while the inside is subjected to heat and fumes. It is, therefore, essential that the flues are lined in order to prevent smoke and fumes from escaping other than through the outlet at the top of the flue. It is good practice to insulate the lining from the brick surround by filling the space between them with a loose material, such as vermiculite, which is resistant to heat and has excellent insulating properties. Figure 7.13 shows the construction of a one-flue chimney stack. Figure 7.15 shows a typical two-flue stack.

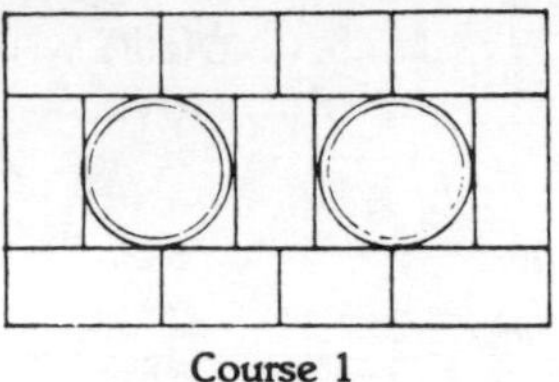

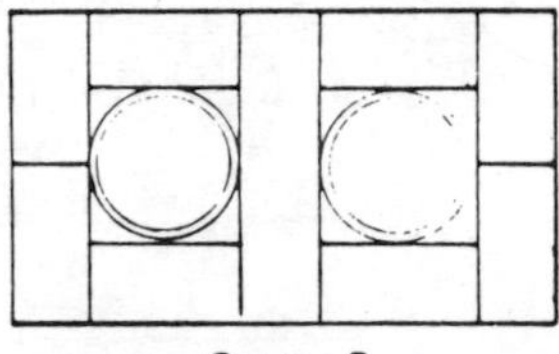

Figure 7.15 A two-flue stack

Flue outlets

The outlet of a flue excluding the chimney pot must be not less than one metre above the highest point of contact between the chimney and the roof. This is shown in Figure 7.16. If the roof has a pitch on each side of the ridge of not less than 10 degrees and the chimney passes through the roof within 600 mm of the ridge, then the chimney must not be less than 600 mm above the ridge.

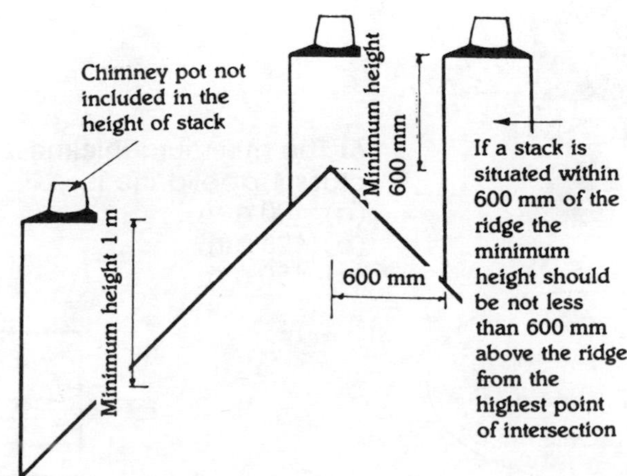

Figure 7.16 The minimum heights of chimney stacks at different positions on the roof

The outlet may be formed by projecting the flue liner at the top of the stack and then finishing it off by *flaunching* around the liner at the top of the brickwork to provide a *weathering*, as shown in Figure 7.17. It is a good practice to build the stack with hard-burnt bricks bedded in a mortar comprised of a mix 1 : 4 of sulphate-resisting cement and sand. However, if ordinary facing bricks are used then the mix should be Portland cement, lime and sand in the ratio, 1 : 1 : 6. The best type of joint finish to a chimney stack is the weather-struck, or weather-struck and cut, as described on p. 62.

In the interests of economy the chimney stack may be built with commons up to the level of the *flashing* (see below), and with facings above the height at which the flashing is dressed into the brickwork.

A more efficient way of finishing the outlet is to build in a chimney pot. This not only gives a better appearance at the top but it also increases the updraught to the flue gases, because the flue narrows off at the top and increases the flow which tends to prevent downdraught. The pot should be well built into the stack to prevent it from becoming dislodged, as shown in Figure 7.17.

Types of chimney pots are shown in Figure 7.18.

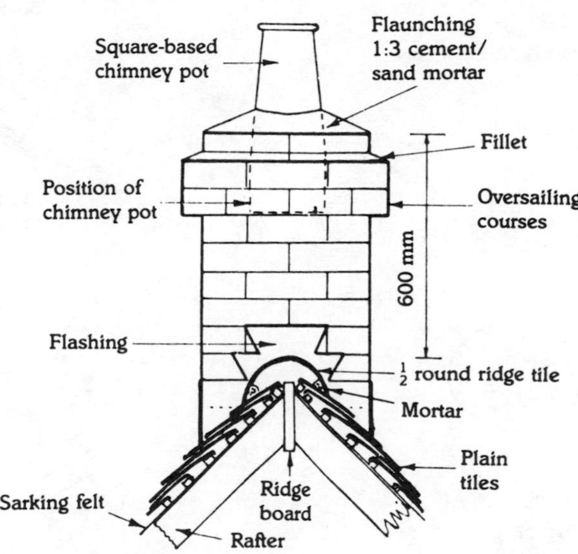

Figure 7.17 A method of building in a chimney pot

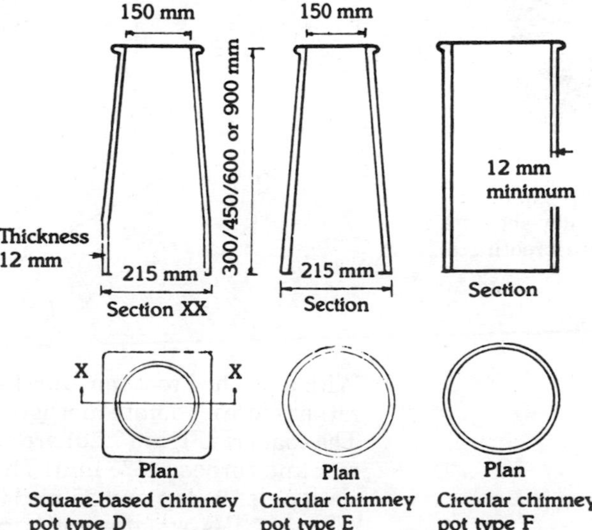

Figure 7.18 Types of chimney pots

Damp prevention in a chimney stack

Chimney stacks are very vulnerable to damp because of their exposed position. In a flat roof the damp proof course should be laid not less than 150 mm above the roof surface and allowed to protrude, and when the roof surface is laid it should be dressed right up to the d.p.c. which is then dressed over the top (Figure 7.19).

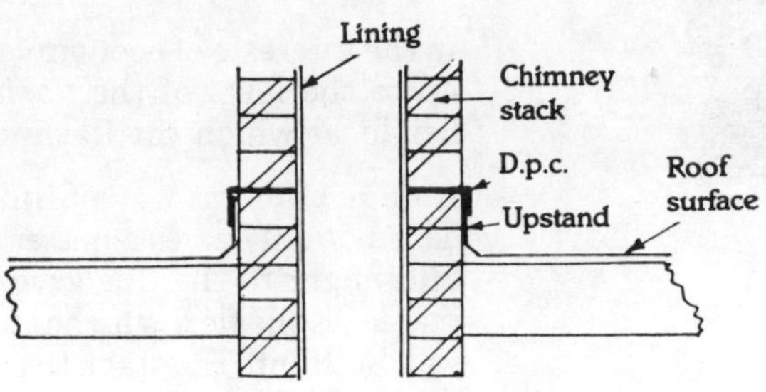

Figure 7.19 Section showing a method of waterproofing a chimney stack where it passes through a flat roof

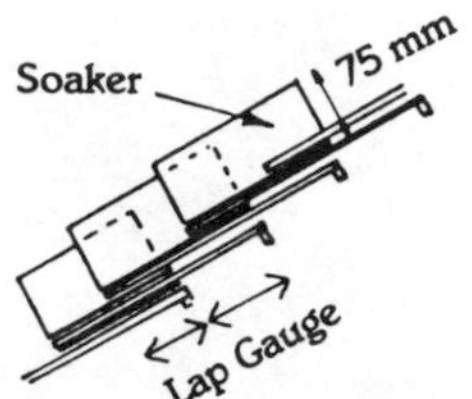

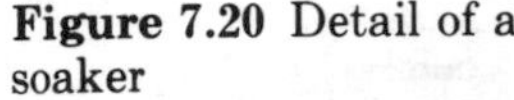

Figure 7.20 Detail of a soaker

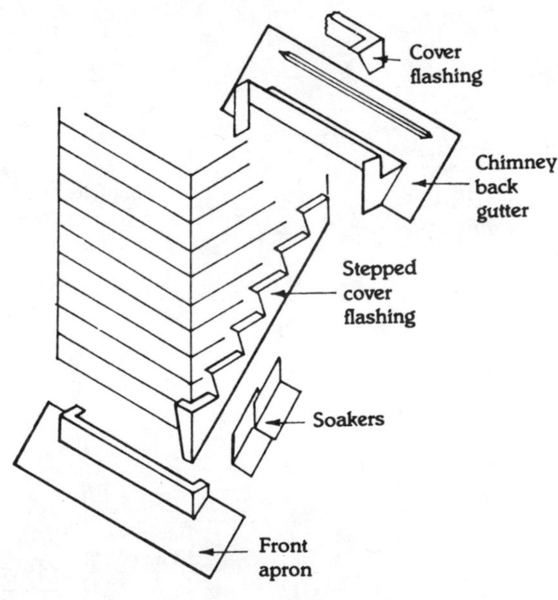

Figure 7.21 An exploded view of a chimney showing a method of waterproofing a chimney stack

With a pitched roof the junction between the roof and the stack requires a rather more elaborate method of waterproofing, as is shown in Figure 7.21. The soakers (Figure 7.20) are cut from a non-ferrous metal such as lead or zinc and turned up 75 mm. Their length is equal to the gauge of the tile or slate plus the lap and 25 mm for fixing. A soaker is placed between each course of tiles or slates and turned up so that it is covered by the flashing.

The flashing is built into the joints of the brickwork, either at one level all round the stack, or in steps, which is called *stepped flashing,* as shown in Figures 7.22, 7.23.

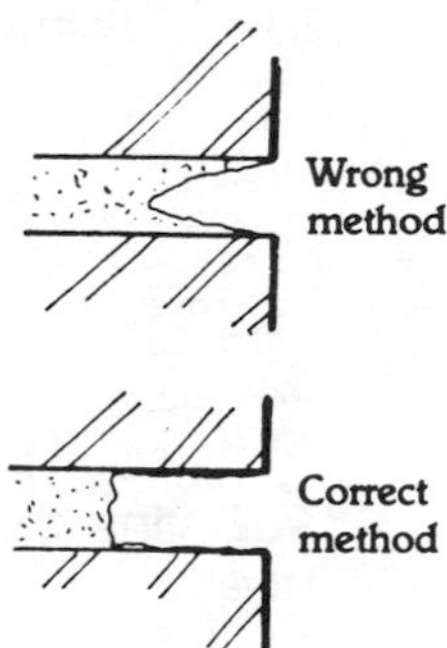

Figure 7.22 Method of raking out bed joints for flashing

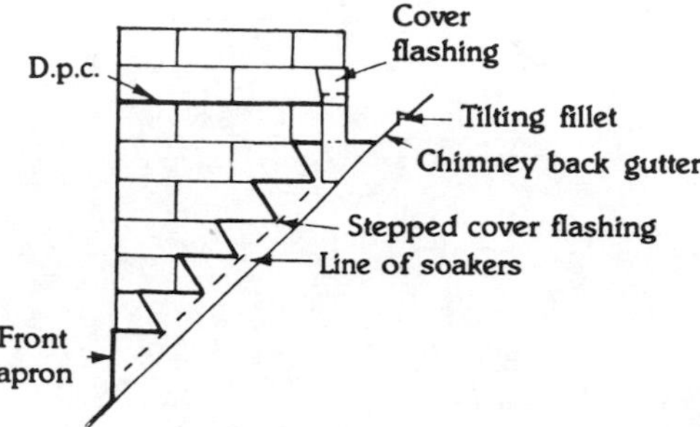

Figure 7.23 Stepped cover flashing

The front of the stack is protected with a front apron and the back of the stack has a back gutter which is sealed with a cover flashing. A d.p.c. is also placed right across the stack to give full protection.

Tolerances

The chimney stack should be plumb ± 3 mm in 1 m height.
The d.p.c. should be correctly positioned at the lower and upper intersections of the roof. All joins and laps should have a minimum lap of 100 mm.
The projection of the corbels should be uniform along the length of the wall ± 3 mm.
The corbels should be level, should not filt forward and have full cross joints.
The chimney pot should be level in both directions ± 2 mm.
The flaunching should be a uniform shape.

Questions for you

7. A chimney stack should project above a roof not less than:
(a) 914 mm
(b) 974 mm
(c) 1 metre

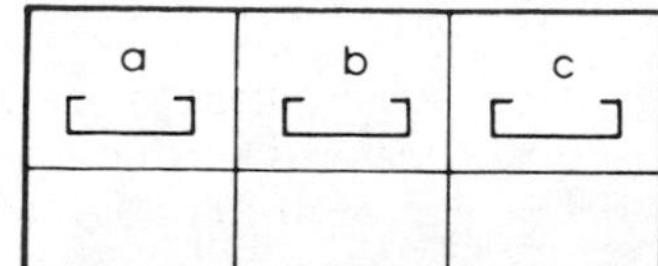

8. A soaker is a piece of sheet metal placed:
(a) between each tile
(b) at the front of the stack to form an apron
(c) at the back of the chimney stack to form a gutter

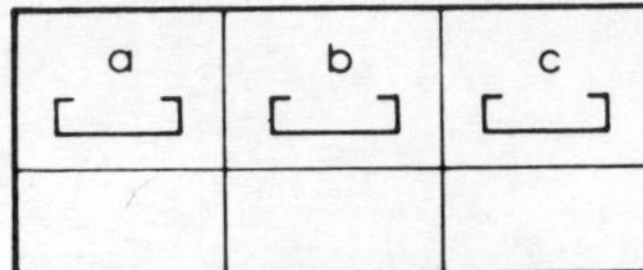

9. Define the term 'flaunching' and explain where it would be used.

____

____

____

Index

Admixtures 12
Aerated concrete blocks 64
Aggregate 11
Air brick 33
Air vent 32, 33, 34, 76, 83–4
Angle of distribution 13
Attached piers 13, 46–7, 58–60, 70
Angle grinder 3
Appliances 3, 87, 89
Apron 96–7
Arris 36
Asphalt 32, 39
Autoclave 9

Back gutter 96–7
Beamfilling 54
Bearing 44
Bevel 53
Bituminous felt 32
Block bonding 20, 68–9
Blockwork 33, 64–73
Boaster 5, 53
Bolster 5, 53
Bonding 13–16
Boot lintel 80–1
Brick core 55
Brick-cutting machinery 3
Brick hammer 6
Brick jointer 7, 62
Brick lifter 10
Brick-on-edge 36–7
Broken bond 49, 67
Building line 30
Buttered joint 37

Calcium silicate bricks 9
Capping 36–8
Cavity batten 75–85
Cavity insulation 85–6
Cavity wall tie 74–5, 85
Cement 9, 11–12, 63, 65, 95
Chimney 87, 94–8
Chimney breast 89–90, 92
Chimney pot 94, 95
Closer 15, 22, 23, 24
Closer gauge 6–7
Club hammer 53
Cold bridge 82
Cold chisel 5
Collar joint 23
Coloured mortar 12, 63
Comb hammer 6
Common bricks 9, 95
Compo 11
Compressive strength 41, 49
Concrete 32, 42, 87, 88
Concrete blocks 33, 65
Concrete bricks 9
Concrete core 42, 55
Coping stone 36, 39
Corbel 95

Coring hole 75
Corner block 6, 7, 19, 69
Corner construction 18–20, 69
Corner profile 19–20, 30
Course 17–20
Cramp 37, 51, 83
Creasing tile 37
Creep 41
Cross joint 14

Damp-prevention course 20, 32–5, 39, 75, 76, 79–82, 84, 88, 95, 96–7
Datum 14–15
Datum peg 14, 15, 18, 20, 67
Dead-man profile 19
Distribution of loading 13
Drip 36
Drying shrinkage 39, 65

Efflorescence 39
Electrical equipment 3
English bond 22–3
English garden-wall bond 26–7
Engineering bricks 9, 32, 83
Exfoliated mica 64
Eye line 37

Face bricks 9
Feather-edge coping 36, 39
Fender wall 88
Fillet 37, 39, 95
Fine aggregate 11, 63
Fireback 90
Fireclay 92
Fixing cramps 51
Flashing 95–7
Flaunching 88, 95
Flemish bond 24–6
Flemish garden-wall bond 27–8
Flettons 9
Flue 87, 88, 92, 94
Flue lining 88, 90–2, 95–6
Flue outlet 95–6
Flush joint 15, 61
Floor construction 32, 34, 76, 84, 88
Fly-ash blocks 52, 64
Formwork 42, 50
Foundation 18, 30, 32, 34, 76

Gable 54
Gauge 14, 45–6
Gauge rod 6, 14, 18, 20, 45–6, 67
Gauging mortar 11, 62–3
Goggles 2
Grinder 3
Grout 36

Half bat 6, 24
Hardcore 32, 76, 88
Hawk 6
Header 9, 15, 17, 22, 23, 26, 46
Hearth 87–90
Helmet 2
Hod 9

Hollow core 55
Honeycomb walling 32, 34
Hoop iron 41
Hydrated lime 11, 63

Indent 20, 68–9
Infill bricks 24–5
Isolated piers 55–7
Insulation 85–6

Jamb 79, 89–90
Joggle joint 36, 64
Jointing 61–3
Jointing iron 7, 62
Junction wall 23–4, 25–6, 27, 28, 47, 68

Lap 15, 22, 96
Lateral strength 13
Leaf 74–5, 79–80, 85
Levelling 15, 17–18
Levelling board 14–15
Lightweight blocks 64
Lime 11, 63, 65
Line 5, 14, 19, 20, 30, 53, 67
Line pin 5, 19, 53, 67
Lintel 43–4, 49–50, 73, 80–3, 88, 90
Load distribution 13

Machine-pressed bricks 9
Masonry cement 11
Mastic sealant 52
Measuring tape 6
Mortar 11
Mortar board 2
Mortar mixers 12
Mortar mixes 11, 55, 62–3, 65, 76, 95
Mortar screed 20, 30, 39, 45
Movement joints 39

Neutral plane 49

Oversite concrete 32, 76, 88

Padstone 44
Parapet wall 36, 39
Partition wall 64, 68
Perpend 14, 15, 22
Pigments 63
Pinch bar 49
Pitch polymer felt 32
Plinth brick 47
Plumbing 14, 17, 30
Pointing trowel 5
Portland cement 11
Profile 19, 20, 30, 61, 68
Protective clothing 2, 3
Purpose-made bricks 36–7

Quetta bond 41–2
Quoin 14, 15, 22–4, 45–6, 69

Raking back 19
Ramp 53–4
Recessed joint 62
Reinforced brickwork 41–2
Reinforced concrete 41–2, 43, 49, 73, 81, 87–9, 90
Reinforcement 41, 43, 49, 68–9
Reveal 79–80
Reverse bond 49
Roofing tile 37, 95
Rounded joint 62
Rule 6

Saddle-back coping 36
Safety 2
Sand 11, 63
Sand courses 20, 52
Sand lime bricks 9
Sectional bond 24, 25
Sill 80
Slate 32, 33, 34
Sleeper wall 32, 34, 76
Slenderness ratio 13
Slice barrow 10
Sloping site 33
Soaker 96–7
Socket 90, 91, 92
Soldier arch 81
Spigot end 90–2
Spirit level 6, 15, 17, 18, 30, 46
Splay 53
Steel beam 44
Steel lintel 43, 81, 82
Steel square 55
Stepped d.p.c. 33
Stepped flashing 96–7
Stone-faced concrete 43
Straightedge 15, 17, 61
Straight joint 14
Stretcher 9, 15, 22, 23, 26, 45, 51
Stretcher bond 45
Struck joint 61
Sulphate-resisting cement 39, 95
Sunken hearth 88

Terracotta blocks 64, 65
Three-quarter bat 15, 22, 24, 25, 46, 47, 49, 58, 59, 69
Threshold 83
Throating 39
Tie brick 15, 23, 24
Tingle 15, 20
Tooled joint 62
Toothing 19, 20
Trowel 5, 30
Tuck jointer 6, 7
Tumbling-in 47

Ventilator 32, 33, 34, 76, 83–4
Vertical d.p.c. 75, 79, 80

Wall joint 23
Wall plate 32, 34, 76, 84, 88
Wall ties 74–5, 79–80, 85
Water bar 80
Weathering 36, 47, 95
Weather-struck joint 61–2, 95
Weephole 76
Welsh arch 33–4
Wire-cut bricks 9
Wooden pads 52
Wooden square 55
Working along a line 19